Multicultural Poster Program

Lisa Lyons Durkin and Deborah E. Dixler

Innovative Learning Publications

Addison-Wesley Publishing Company

Menlo Park, California ● Reading, Massachusetts ● New York ● Don Mills, Ontario
Wokingham, England ● Amsterdam ● Bonn ● Paris ● Milan
Madrid ● Sydney ● Singapore ● Tokyo ● Seoul ● Taipei ● Mexico City ● San Juan

Dedications

To Alan, Scott, and Hillary—my wonderful family
To Nina and John—my wonderful "work" family *DED*

To Emily Hunter Ruppert, who taught me that self-esteem is the birthright of *every* child; and
To Jenny, who shows me every day that a child with self-esteem can truly light up the world *LLD*

Consultants

Peggy Ruth Cole, Ph. D.
Director, Program Planning and Development
New York Hall of Science, New York, NY

Judy David, Ed. D.
Early Childhood Consultant, Washington, DC

Kathy Faggella
Child Development Associate (CDA) Advisor
Stratford, CT

Mary Fitzpatrick
Teacher, Rainbow Montessori School,
Madison, NJ

Karen Liu, Ph. D.
Associate Professor of Early Childhood Education
Indiana State University, Terre Haute, IN

Jeannine Perez, Ph. D.
Special Education Teacher, Metcalf School
Normal, IL

This book is published by Innovative Learning Publications ™, an imprint of the Alternative Publishing Group of Addison-Wesley Publishing Company.

Senior Editor: Lois Fowkes
Design Coordinator: Jeff Kelly
Production Coordinator: Karen Edmonds
Poster and Book Design: Nina and John Woldin, Deborah E. Dixler
Illustrations: Deborah E. Dixler, Nina Woldin, Claudine K. Brown, Lisa Schustak, Catherine Minor
Copy Editor: Helen Strahinich
Research: Claudia Ocello, Mary Beth Spann Minucci, Alyssa Levy, Aviva Richman

Contents

Acknowledgments

We gratefully acknowledge the following people and organizations for their information and support on the content of this program:
African National Congress, Washington, DC; Asian American Civic Association, Inc., Boston, MA; Armine Bagdasarian; John Bishai, Arabic Consultants, Cambridge, MA; Joan Bronspiegel; Claudine K. Brown; Doerte Buss, The Boston Public Library; The Children's Museum, Boston, MA; Judith Cooke-Tucker, World Music Press; Crossroads, Madison, NJ; Carol Daily, Country School, Weston, MA; Polly Eberhardt, Co-Director, the F. M. Kirby Children's Center of the Madison Area YMCA, Madison, NJ; Jenelle Erickson, Director, Rainbow Montessori School, Madison, NJ; Bayla Falber; Jana Harchar, Northslope Borough Commission on Inupiat History, Language, and Culture; Nina Jensen, Director, Museum Education Programs, Bank Street College of Education; Korean Travel Bureau; Dr. Margery A. Kranyik, Bridgewater State College, MA; Deborah Lotus, Talking Drum; Ziva Maskowitz, Solomon Schecter Day School, West Orange, NJ; Saara Minnevich, Jewish Community Center, West Orange, NJ; The Morris Museum, Morristown, NJ; Patricia Murray, Brooklake Elementary School, Florham Park, NJ; The Navajo Tribe Nation; The Newark Museum, Newark, NJ; Newark Museum Lending Collection; The Oneida Nation Council; Elizabeth Pendry, Country School; Linda Pickelny, Brooklake School; Kei Sakayama; Grace Shukri, Harvard University Center for Middle Eastern Studies; The Sioux Nation Council; Bill and Diane Smith; Isabelle Spadavecchia, Brooklake School; Gail Willett, Savanna Books; Vishnu Wood, Safari East Multicultural Presentations; Joanne Yovanovich, Skidegate Band Council, Haida Nation

We would like to thank the Consulates and Embassies of the following countries for their time and information:
People's Republic of China, Egypt, France, Ghana, Greece, India, Israel, Italy, Japan, Kenya, Korea, Mexico, Nigeria, Poland, Russia, Saudi Arabia, Sierra Leone, Spain, South Africa, Sweden, Thailand, Vietnam

We would like to acknowledge and thank the following people and organizations for their technical support on this program:
Beth Bispham; Betty Lacy, Brian Lacy, Kathy Culler and Gail Hall, Info X, Inc., Madison, NJ; Dana Nolletti; Dave Smith, Maikron Publishing Center, Florham Park, NJ.

Preface

What is a *multicultural classroom*? What does it look like? How do people act in it?

Before we could begin to develop a program to meet the needs of the multicultural classroom, we needed to be able to observe multicultural education in action for ourselves. And so we visited many classrooms, talked with many teachers, attended many workshops, and read lots of books and articles. We drew on our experience as editors at First Teacher Press, our teaching experience, and work in the field of museum education.

What we concluded is that first and foremost, the multicultural classroom is a place where every child is valued for his or her unique contribution to the class. This concept fits in perfectly with the belief that has always been our guiding principle at First Teacher: the most important learning tool a child has is a positive self-image. Self-esteem has been the underlying theme in all of our publications, and *The Multicultural Poster Program* is no exception.

The multicultural classroom is a place where cultural diversity is valued at all times. In a multicultural classroom, children are encouraged to share their favorite music, stories, games, recipes—all in an atmosphere of acceptance. We hope that the *Multicultural Poster Program* will help to enhance this atmosphere. We hope that the activities in the Teacher's Guide will invite children and their families to bring part of their cultural heritage into the classroom with the assurance that whatever they bring will be treated with interest and respect.

The multicultural classroom is a place where children are taught to acknowledge and respect both similarities and differences. We anticipate that the posters and related activities will open up lively discussions about diversity. We hope that children will come to realize that the similarities they share with classmates and with children around the world form a universal bond, and that the differences they find among individuals and cultures will enrich their lives.

We created the posters in this program to enhance multicultural education in any classroom. The posters have been designed to be integrated into almost any everyday curriculum. They offer pictures of children of various racial and ethnic backgrounds, examples of languages spoken in many countries around the world, and items from a wide variety of cultures. We believe that young children learn best from hands-on experiences and we hope that students will be given the opportunity to interact with the posters and use the pictures as springboards to more concrete experiences with people and objects in their everyday lives. For example, we hope that children will learn about a large assortment of shoes when they explore the Japanese sandal, the *geta*. We encourage you to let children try several different kinds of paper cutting and folding when they study the Polish art of paper cutting, *wycinanki*.

We believe that every classroom has the potential to be a multicultural classroom. However, we acknowledge that in some schools, the students and their families cannot bring cultural diversity into the classroom. In these classrooms, where everyone comes from a similar background and shares a common cultural heritage, the *Multicultural Poster Program* can introduce children to the wider world and encourage them to explore other cultures. First children will discover what they have in common with other cultures—people all over the world greet each other; almost everyone wears some form of foot coverings and head coverings, plays games, and enjoys treats. Then children will explore new ways to say "hello," interesting new shoes and hats, intriguing new games, and tasty new treats.

The key ingredient in any multicultural classroom is the people who spend their time there—the teachers, the children, and family members and other classroom visitors. We expect that the *Multicultural Poster Program* will be used in different ways in different classroom. The *Around the World Greetings Poster* is most effective when it reflects the linguistic heritage of everyone in the class. Children will take full advantage of the *Around the World from A to Z Poster* when they use the pictures of unfamiliar items as inspiration to explore objects with similar functions in their own world.

We believe that all children deserve to feel good about themselves in all aspects including cultural roots and heritage. It follows that they also need to be respectful and appreciative of the cultural roots of others. We hope that the *Multicultural Poster Program* will help children and teachers to achieve this end.

Introduction

Overview

The *Multicultural Poster Program* is a supplementary early childhood program for children five to eight years old that will help you weave multicultural themes into your existing curriculum. The program uses similarities among people around the world as a basis for exploring and appreciating cultural differences. It consists of four full-color posters and this Teacher's Guide. The Guide offers extensive suggestions for tailoring the posters and related activities to the specific needs and interests of your class.

The program themes are age-appropriate and geared to the interests of young children (for example, friends, toys and games, food, animals, and folktales). These themes can be integrated into many content areas, including science, math, whole language, art, music and movement, and cooking. By taking part in the program, children will develop an understanding and appreciation of their own heritage that comes from sharing that heritage with others. They will also learn about and gain respect for other cultures.

Components

Around the World Map: This poster is a large, colorful map of the world. Continents are defined with bold, simple outlines and colors, countries by thin lines. Place names are not shown on the map. An annotated map is available in this Guide for easy reference. You may use this interactive poster in many ways during the year. It is strongly recommended that a globe also be available in the classroom near the map for reference and comparison.

I'm Special Poster: This poster features photographs of children from a variety of racial and ethnic backgrounds engaged in activities familiar to young school children. The photographs form a frame, leaving space in the center of the poster where you can highlight individual class members. This poster can be used as the backdrop for a "Child of the Week" display. The Guide focuses on how to integrate multiculturalism into a "Child of the Week" theme, and includes a Letter to Parents as well as instructions for an "All About Me" collage. This poster encourages children to explore similarities and differences in a positive way. It also can be a springboard to discussions of cultural diversity within a classroom.

Greetings Poster: This poster features examples of many of the world's major languages and alphabets. Each word or phrase expresses a greeting. You can create a truly representative multicultural display for your classroom by adding around the border of the poster greetings in other languages, written on file cards by parents, school staff, and visitors.

Around the World from A to Z: This poster presents 26 items, one for each letter of the alphabet. These items are chosen from many of the major cultures found in the United States and around the world. They provide a concrete, age-appropriate way for children to explore cultural similarities and differences. Large black-and-white illustrations of the items appear in the Guide.

Teacher's Guide: The Guide contains activities, projects, recipes, songs, stories, children's literature suggestions, and reference materials for teachers, all related to the posters.

Tips for Teaching

- The *Multicultural Poster Program* is a supplementary program, not a curriculum. The posters need not be used in the sequence presented in the Guide to be effective. Each unit presents a variety of activities from which to choose. Survey the program and then integrate parts of it into your existing curriculum in segments that meet the needs of your class.

- Your students should be your first resource in discussions of themes and objects. Whenever possible, begin your introduction to a new or unusual item or concept with a reference to children's first-hand experiences. For example, invite children to talk about the kinds of bread they like before introducing *baguettes.* Let children describe games they enjoy before your introduction to *valero* and *tiu-ü.*

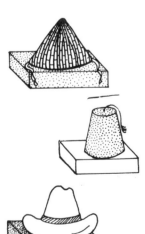

- Your best resources for multicultural information and hands-on experiences are the families of your students. Make families aware of your interest in their heritage through letters like the ones on pages 25, 35, and 47, and during parent/teacher meetings, workshops, and family get-togethers at school. Involve volunteers whenever possible, and encourage parents who cannot come to school to send in cultural items for children to explore and foods for them to taste. (Whenever you cook with children or give them something unusual to taste, be aware of individual allergies and dietary restrictions.)

- Use community resources to supplement the cultural diversity of your class. Borrow objects of interest from lending collections at libraries and museums. Use ethnic clubs and foreign student associations at local colleges and universities to locate potential class visitors with first-hand knowledge of other cultures. Invite foreign-language students from local high schools and colleges to come to your class and share interesting information about the cultures they are studying and to teach your children words and phrases from other languages.

- Don't be afraid to change the focus of a lesson if it better suits your student population and available resources. For example, if you are doing a lesson from the *A to Z Poster* on *non la,* a Vietnamese hat, and a child has brought in a similar hat from another culture, discuss the idea that wide-brimmed hats are worn in other places for the same reason they are worn in Vietnam—to protect people from the hot sun. Then satisfy your children's curiosity about other aspects of life in that other culture with books, visitors, and so on. Be sure to discuss all the hats that children like to wear.

- Set up multicultural exhibits on familiar themes. A display might tie into items on the *A to Z Poster* such as hats, shoes, or musical instruments, or it might highlight your students' countries of origin.

   To create an exhibit, set aside a table or the top of a book shelf. Cover it with a plain bed sheet, piece of fabric, or felt. If possible, cover some small boxes with cloth for displaying objects at different heights. Place a label in front of each object identifying the object, the name of the owner, and the object's country of origin. Small objects might be placed in shoe boxes (or larger boxes) to make dioramas. Children can draw backgrounds for the objects and then place the drawings in the box. They can add clay figures and twig trees where appropriate to the scene.

   Invite children to make a mural on the multicultural theme. For example, each child might draw herself in her favorite hat for a hat exhibit.

   Let children make a large, colorful sign for the exhibit; for example, "Hats Around the World." Then set up viewing times for the exhibit and rules for what items may and may not be touched. To make the exhibit interactive, encourage children to notice details in the objects. Encourage children to gently handle objects whenever possible, in order to explore textures and shapes. Try to have a magnifying glass available for children to use.

   If possible, move your exhibit into a hall showcase so that the whole school can enjoy it or invite other classes to visit your classroom.

- If possible, create a permanent multicultural bulletin board area in your class room with space around the posters to add items of interest and children's artwork that relate to multicultural themes.

- Laminating the posters will make them sturdier and help them last longer.

- If you do not have wall space in your classroom for the four posters, you might wish to create a flip chart that could be stored in an accessible closet and brought out whenever you do part of the program. You'll need an easel and a large piece of cardboard at least 23 by 35 inches. Attach the posters to the cardboard with clipboard-style clips. You can rearrange the posters, depending on which lessons you are teaching.

- Because the posters are full of interesting items to explore, you may wish to use a framing device to help children focus on one item or group of items. As an example, you could create a masking frame by cutting a square or rectangle out of a large piece of oaktag. Place the poster item you wish to highlight in the window and mask the items around it with the oaktag.

Cultural Overview

Africa

Asia

Australia

Europe

North America

South America

Content Area Chart

	Math	Science	Whole Language	Art	Cooking	Social Studies	Children's Literature	Music
Around the World Map	X	X	X			X	X	
I'm Special	X		X	X	X	X	X	
Around the World Greetings	X	X	X	X		X	X	
Around the World from A to Z:								
Anansi		X	X	X		X	X	
Baguette		X			X	X	X	
Castanets				X		X	X	X
Dream catcher		X	X	X		X	X	
Elephant	X	X				X	X	
Fry bread				X	X	X	X	
Geta	X		X	X		X	X	
Hop-round	X					X	X	
Ibheque			X	X		X	X	
Junk			X		X	X	X	
Kiondo				X		X	X	
Lebkuchen			X	X	X	X	X	
Matroshka dolls	X		X	X		X	X	
Non la			X	X		X	X	
Ofrenda pictures	X			X		X	X	
Palay					X	X	X	
Qamutig		X	X	X		X	X	
Raven			X	X		X	X	
Shekere		X		X		X	X	X
Tiu-ü	X			X		X	X	
'Ud				X		X	X	X
Valero	X			X		X	X	
Wycinanki	X			X		X	X	
Xylophone			X			X	X	X
Yeon		X	X	X		X	X	
Zampoña		X				X	X	X

Around the World Map

Poster Activities

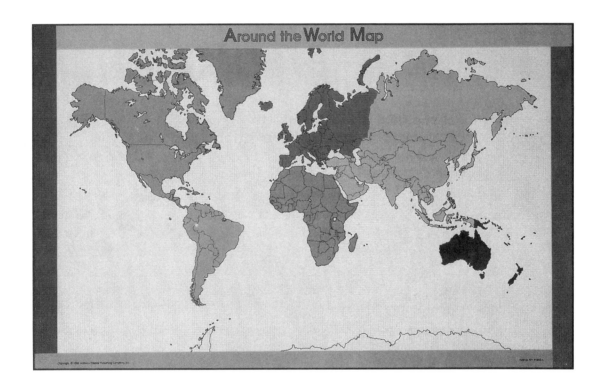

Key to Continents
in Around the World Map Poster

North America- green
South America- orange
Europe-   red
Africa-   dark blue
Asia-   yellow
Australia-   purple
Antarctica-   tan

Countries highlighted in
Multicultural Poster Progam

North America
1. Canada
2. United States of America
3. Mexico
4. Guatemala
5. Panama
6. Puerto Rico

South America
7. Colombia
8. Ecuador
9. Peru
10. Bolivia

Europe
11. Portugal
12. Spain
13. Ireland
14. United Kingdom
15. France
16. Belgium
17. Netherlands
18. Germany
19. Austria
20. Poland
21. Sweden
22. Estonia
23. Italy
24. Greece

Africa
25. Guinea
26. Sierra Leone
27. Liberia
28. Ghana
29. Nigeria
30. Congo
31. Angola
32. South Africa
33. Zimbabwe
34. Malawi
35. Kenya
36. Egypt

Asia
37. Israel
38. Lebanon
39. Turkey
40. India
41. Thailand
42. Malaysia
43. Cambodia
44. Laos
45. Vietnam
46. Hong Kong
47. China
48. North Korea
49. South Korea
50. Japan
51. Philippines
52. Russia

53. **Australia**

Overview

Background Information

Children in the primary grades are just beginning to learn about maps and to develop mapping skills. Maps and globes are too abstract for most young children to really understand. Therefore throughout this program, the *World Map* will act as a place to display and classify the information children gather about cultures. This information will include photographs, illustrations, words, and phrases. It will be a visual reference for children and a place where they can make connections among language, objects, stories, and ideas. Children will begin to form a picture of the countries where certain foods they enjoy, toys they play with, and folktales they listen to originated.

Each of the seven continents is a different color on the *World Map,* and the national borders are defined with black lines. The map has no place names that might distract or confuse children. For your reference, there is an annotated version of the map on pages 14-15. You can customize the *World Map* with the names of places you feel that your children should know or with names they wish to learn.

The *World Map* is designed to be an integral part of your classroom. In this unit there are suggestions for using this poster independently or in conjunction with the other three posters in the program. Even if your children come from similar backgrounds, they will able to experience being part of a wider world when you use the map to classify local ethnic restaurants, folktales and realistic multicultural stories, TV programs set in faraway locales, newspaper and magazine stories, visitors who speak different languages, objects and foods from other countries, and so on.

Objectives

* To introduce the concept that the world is a large place
* To help children explore the concepts of *near* and *far away*
* To help children become aware of the many multicultural influences that touch their lives

Materials

World Map, globe, string, tape or thumbtacks, file cards or sticky-back notes

Introduction

Before you introduce the *World Map*, spend some time with children looking at a globe. This may be a first introduction to a globe for younger children; older students may have had prior experience with globes or maps they can share with the group. Depending on the age and experience level of your children, you might ask questions, such as:

• What is this object?
• What do we use a globe for?
• What shape is the globe?
• What do you think the areas of blue might represent on the globe?

Explain that the earth is a sphere. Talk about other objects children know that are spheres—balls, oranges, marbles, and so on. Let children feel the curved surface of the globe.

Now show children the *World Map*. Tell them this poster represents what a globe might look like if it were flat. Help children match the shapes of the continents and large bodies of water on the globe to areas on the map.

Find the approximate location of your state on the *World Map*. Identify it by attaching a small photo of your school or your class on the side of the map and connecting it to the location with string. Tell children that throughout the year the map will be a center for items and information that they will collect about different countries and groups of people.

Some of the children in your class or their families may have come from other places in the world. Use the map to show your students where these places are and how far they are from your state. As an example, show children one country in the world where your ancestors lived, which you have visited, or where you have friends. Place a sticky-back note with your name on it on that country on the map. Ask questions, such as:

• What kind of transportation might I use to travel to _____ for a visit?
• Would I use a plane, a boat, a car, a train, some other kind of transportation, or all of these?
• How would I get to _____ ? (Have children take turns tracing a possible route on the map with their fingers.)

Invite other school personnel, visitors, and parents to add information to countries on the poster. Some children may also wish to locate the countries of their ancestors as they become more familiar with their own cultural backgrounds. Others may only be familiar with the United States as their ancestors' country of origin. Be sure to validate each child's perception of his background.

Working with the Posters

The *World Map* is designed to be used in conjunction with the other posters in the program. A variety of activities which make use of the *World Map* will be described in detail in later chapters. They include:

I'm Special Poster:
* Recording the ancestries of grandparents and other relatives and friends that your children interview.

Greetings Poster:
* Posting foreign greetings (pages 40-44) on areas of the world where those languages are spoken.
* Posting snapshots of "artwork" pen pals on the map.

A to Z Poster:
* Posting copies of black-and-white illustrations (pages 100-125) around the map and attach them to appropriate areas with string.
* Recording items brought by children from home to supplement those on the poster on the map.
* Posting a copy of the book icon (see below) with the title of a book or story about another culture on the side of the poster and connecting it to the appropriate location with string.

Every few weeks at group time, review the *World Map* with children. Discuss new information you have added to the map and how this information helps to give a clearer picture of how people live around the world and how your life experience is affected by other cultures.

Follow-Up Activities

Children's Literature

Books and Folktales: Whenever you read a story that takes place in another part of the world or involves characters with different cultural backgrounds, use the book icon (see preceding page) and post the title on the map. Children may wish to add books from outside of school as well. Encourage them to share multicultural stories they have enjoyed at home or at the library. Always relate the story or character to other facts you know about the culture. If you have introduced the *Greetings Poster*, you might ask: *"How might Jose* (character in the story) *greet his grandmother?"* (*"¡Hola!"*)

Social Studies

Community Resources: Encourage children to bring in pictures, brochures, menus, and so on when they visit different community locations. These may include restaurants, food markets, museums, houses of worship, and community fairs. Post the items on the bulletin board around the map.

Postcards: Use postcards to learn about different locations on the *World Map*. If you have the space on your wall, you can create a frame of postcards around the map. Children can use postcards to compare different locations. Most children will be amazed at the geographic variety, even within the United States, from desert to mountains, from large cities to farmlands. Ask questions to help children focus on the details in the picture. What is the weather in the picture? How can you tell? What are the people doing in the picture? Are their clothes for everyday wear or are they for a special occasion? Do children dress differently from adults? If so, how? Are there houses in the picture? If so, what do they tell you about how these people live? Are there stores? What is sold in the stores? Children may become so intrigued by a postcard that you may want to bring them more information about the location through books, brochures, or even a visit with the person who sent or received the postcard.

You have a variety of resources to help you collect postcards. You can ask families to bring back postcards when they travel. You can ask your own friends and relatives in other places to send cards. Classroom parents can do the same thing with their friends and relatives. You can write to a school in another location and ask if their students would like to exchange postcards with yours. Travel agencies often get postcards and may be willing to give them to your class. You can also request cards from visitors' bureaus of other cities or states or consulates of different countries.

Magazines: Cut pictures of different locations, people in different kinds of clothing, interesting animals, and art objects from magazines such as *National Geographic, Travel and Leisure*, and so on.

Extending the Theme

Books for Children

Have available one or more children's atlases, such as *Rand McNally Children's Atlas* and *The Reader's Digest Children's Atlas,* for children to explore. Often these books contain pictures and information about different cultures.

Maps and Globes, by Caroline Arnold (Franklin Watts), gives an introduction to the uses of maps and globes and tells how to make a balloon globe, a model of a room, a giant compass rose, and more.

Second Treasury of the World's Greatest Fairytales, by Helen Hyman (Danbury Press), is an extensive collection of fairytales from around the world.

South and North, East and West, edited by Michael Rosen (Oxfam), is a collection of folktales from around the world.

Tales from Many Lands Papercrafts, by Jerome Brown (Fearon), features tales from many cultures and puppets you can make to enhance storytelling.

Talking Walls, by Margy Burns (Tilbury House), tells about walls around the world and how they are used.

This Is the Way We Go to School, by Edith Bauer (Scholastic), is a book featuring different ways children travel to school around the world.

I'm Special

Poster Activities

# Overview

Background Information

As children can begin to explore their cultural roots, they need to become aware of their own value as individuals. It is also important that every child recognize and appreciate ways in which others are alike and different from him. It is a challenge as a teacher to create a balance between encouraging a sense of community and helping each child to contribute his special qualities and experiences to the group. Remember that all children must feel liked and accepted before they can like and accept others.

The *I'm Special Poster* is designed to help children explore the similarities and differences among young children of many racial and ethnic backgrounds. Children in your class will have the opportunity to discover what they have in common with the children on the poster. They will be able to explore any differences they see.

The poster can serve as a frame for each child's uniqueness, the expression of which may take many forms. Each child in your class should have the opportunity to make the center section of the poster "his own" at some point during the year, either with an "All About Me" collage (see directions on pages 23-24), photographs, or other personal items. This poster can spotlight "The Child of the Week" or act as a backdrop for personal exhibits by class members. You may wish to laminate this poster for durability.

Many of the activities in this unit will also help you learn more about your children's families and their cultural backgrounds. Once a child and his family feel truly a part of your "classroom family," they will feel more comfortable sharing the objects, language, foods, and traditions that are part of their heritage.

Objectives

- To develop the awareness that people are alike in many ways
- To develop the awareness that people are different in many ways
- To help children appreciate the fact that we are all unique and special in our looks, our actions, and our interests
- To develop the awareness that young children in different locations enjoy the same kinds of activities in school

Materials

Construction paper, old magazines, collage materials, scissors, glue, thumbtacks or drafting tape, *I'm Special Poster,* copies of page 25 (one per child)

Introduction

Teacher "All About Me" Collage: Help children need to feel comfortable about sharing their personal thoughts and ideas by sharing some information about yourself. One way to do this is to make an "All About Me" collage, telling about you, the teacher. Children will see that it's OK to share information about themselves, and they will also have guidelines to follow when it is their turn to make an "All About Me" collage. Make sure that children understand that your collage is unique and not a model that they have to copy.

Materials: 9-by-12-inch construction paper in different colors; old magazines; collage materials such as fabric scraps, wallpaper books, paint color chips; scissors; glue; markers or crayons

What to Do:

1. Choose a piece of construction paper in your favorite color.
2. On the paper, create a collage to show things that you like. If possible, invite groups of children to help you with choosing collage materials and gluing. Here are some ideas:
- Use different collage materials to show textures, patterns, shapes, and colors that you like.
- Cut out magazine pictures to show foods, places, activities, famous people, animals, or anything that you particularly like or that give information that want to share about yourself.
- Try to include in the collage a few photos of yourself at different ages as well as pictures of family, friends, pets, and favorite places.
- Add original artwork to the collage, if it is appropriate, perhaps a self-portrait, drawing of a pet, or scene that you like.
- Glue on tickets from special events, postcards from places you have visited, and wrappers from favorite foods.
3. Display your completed "All About Me" collage in the center of the *I'm Special Poster*. Help children will learn more about you by asking them questions such as: *"What might this (picture, item) on the collage tell you about me?"*

Use these directions as a guideline to making children's "All About Me" collages. This activity should be done by each child at some time during the year, possibly when she is being highlighted as "Child of the Week."

Make copies of the letter on page 25 to send home to parents to tell them what you are doing and to request their contributions. This letter can be sent home when the child is preparing to make the collage, so families can help their child decide what to include. If children are expected to collect items for their collages over a long period of time, give them file folders or manila envelopes in which to store their collections. Depending on how you integrate the activity into your existing curriculum, you may wish to work on the collages one-on-one with each child or in small groups. You might even have children complete the project at home and then bring it to school.

Working with the Posters

Children will be introduced to the *I'm Special Poster* when you display your "All About Me" collage in the center of the poster. Use drafting tape to hang the collage so that the poster will not tear when you take it down. (If drafting tape is unavailable, use two thumbtacks to hang up the collage. When you take it down, put clear tape over the thumbtack holes to prevent tearing. Use the same holes to hang children's collages.)

Highlight each child or group of children in the montage of photos on the *I'm Special* poster. Many of the scenes relate to multicultural experiences in this book. Help your students describe the various activities children in the poster are engaged in (clockwise from upper left hand corner): playing with matroshka dolls (see pages 72-73 for more information and activities about these dolls); reading a Big Book (see page 54); looking at a globe (see page 17); preparing bread dough (see pages 50-51 and 58-59); playing with a puppet; walking on a balance beam; playing musical instruments: shekere (see pages 84-85), xylophone (see pages 94-95), rhythm sticks; playing with dominoes (see pages 86-87); creating ofrenda pictures with yarn (see pages 76-77); playing hopscotch (see pages 62-63).

As children explore the poster, ask questions such as the following:
* How do you think the children in the poster are feeling about the activities they are doing?
* What do you like to do during art time? What do you like to do during cooking time? What about music time?
* What is your favorite book? Where do you like to sit when you look at books?
* What games do you like to play when you are sitting down?
* What games do you know that require hopping?

You may wish to take a vote or make a graph to see which activity among those on the poster your children find most interesting. Students could also add other activities they enjoy to the chart.

Use the children in the poster to explore in a positive way physical similarities and differences with the students in your class. Let students point out characteristics the poster models share with each other or that your children share with them.

Dear Parents,

This year your child will be making an "All About Me" collage. A collage is created by pasting a variety of special items and pictures on construction paper. Through their collages, children will have the opportunity to share people, places, and objects that they especially enjoy and that, taken together, make them special and tell about them. In the "All About Me" collage, your child will have the opportunity to highlight interests, activities, hobbies, preferences—anything that he or she enjoys or cares about.

We hope you will help your child find examples of the following and bring them into class on:

_____

* favorite foods (pictures, labels)
* things your child likes to do (games, sports, home activities)
* things your child like to collect (cards, stickers, photographs)
* photographs of family, friends, pets, home
* postcards from trips, family or friends who live far away, places your child would like to visit
* tickets, ads, brochures, menus from favorite places
* anything that tells about your child and that can be cut up and pasted

Your child's "All About Me" collage will be on display on

_____

Please drop by to see it.

Sincerely,

Follow-Up Activities

Whole Language

Name Signs: Encourage children to ask their families why they were given their names. Then use books, such as *The Melting Pot Book of Baby Names*, by Connie Lockhart Ellefson (Betterway Publications), to help interested children learn more about their names. You can tell a child where his first name came from and show him the place on the *World Map*. Then tell him the meaning of the name. You can share variations on a common name; for example: John, Jan, Sean, Juan, Johannes, and so on. You may want to use more than one reference book, since meanings can differ. Some names may not have meanings in books, so you may have to ask parents to share the family history of the name or another reason why they chose that name.

Let children write their first names on large paper plates, construction paper, or oaktag, either with markers or with glue and glitter, and then illustrate the name with pictures or designs they like. If a child is named after a family member, he might also want to add a picture of that person to his name sign. These signs can be used to identify cubbies or private places at home.

"All About Me" Exhibit: This exhibit is a three-dimensional variation on the "All About Me" collage. Tell families that each child needs a shoebox, which will be the foundation of the exhibit. Have parents and children gather items that can be glued to the outside of the box. Each item must be one that tells something about the child. Children can put in the box photos of themselves, family members, friends, pets, and special places; postcards or pictures of places they have visited; small items that depict hobbies and interests, such as baseball cards and stickers; and souvenirs and brochures of favorite places to visit. Children can choose other items to be placed inside the box: a favorite stuffed animal, doll, or action figure; a game; an article of clothing; packaged food; or sports equipment that tells something important about the child. The possibilities are endless. Have children describe the contents of their "All About Me" Exhibits at sharing time and then put the box on display for everyone to view. Set ground rules: no touching; only looking.

Cooking

A Recipe for Me: This activity combines cooking and creative expression.

Materials: ingredients and materials necessary for making the lebkuchen recipe on page 111, paper, markers or crayons

What to Do:

1. Make gingerbread people with children, using the cookie recipe on page 111 or your favorite recipe. As you cook, talk about the ingredients and measurements.

2. As the cookies are baking, discuss with children how all of us are made of different "ingredients." There could be a "recipe" for each of us. Give as an example a recipe for yourself: one cup of brown hair, two blue eyes, one nose, a teaspoon of freckles, 5 cups of laughter, and so on.

3. Give each child a sheet of paper. You may wish to trace the shape of a cookie-cutter person on one side of the paper. Challenge children to draw themselves as a cookie and then to write or dictate the ingredients they would contain.

4. When the cookies are done, let everyone decorate them with icing and raisins and enjoy them as children share the "Recipes for Me" that they have created.

Math

Grouping and Graphing: Give children concrete experiences with similarities and differences by playing the following game. First, have children stand in groups according to their hair color: brown, blond, red, and black. Make sure that each child is standing in a group. Regroup children several times according to different criteria: eye color, colors of clothing, beginning letter of their first name, birthday month, and so on. You can invite children to make up additional catagories. Make sure that every child belongs to some group when you change criteria. Point out to children that everyone belongs to a number of groups, each of which has different members. For the last criterion, name a characteristic shared by all the children, such as everyone younger than seven years old, everyone who lives in (name of town), or everyone who likes playing games.

Create pictographs with children, charting eye color, hair color, and /or texture (straight or curly). Use pictures of eyes or heads with hair to symbolize each child on the graph. Help children learn to read the charts by asking questions, such as:

• How many people have brown hair?

• Do more people have blue eyes or brown eyes? (Let children count to find out the answer.)

You can graph the boys and girls separately to make even more comparisons.

curly	straight
	Don
	Sue
Steve	Mag
Maria	John
Betsy	Ben
Jim	Tom

Art

"All About Me" Puppets: Make life-sized tracings of your children. Then bring this project to life by turning each tracing into a life-sized puppet that can sit in a chair or dance around with the help of a young puppeteer.

Materials: butcher paper or sheets of mural-sized paper, markers or crayons, paint, scissors, stapler or glue, old newspapers, paper plates

What to Do:

1. Trace children's bodies on large pieces of paper.
2. Place another sheet under the tracing and cut out two outlines.
3. Have children add personal details to one of the outlines. Let them mix colors of paint to create their skin and hair colors and the colors of their clothes. After paint is dry, encourage children to add facial features. They may want to mix a special eye color as well.
4. Use glue or a stapler to attach the two outlines around the edges. As the outlines are being glued or stapled, let children crush newspaper and stuff the puppet head and body.
5. Cut paper plates in half. Staple half a paper plate upside down onto the back of the puppet's head so that a child's hand can slip into it.

Extending the Theme

Social Studies

Remember that in all of these family-oriented activities a child's family can be any group of people that love and support the child. Anyone a child wishes to include in his family circle should be welcomed at school.

Family Interviews: This activity will help children—and you—get to know parents, grandparents, and even great-grandparents better, opening up avenues for multicultural exploration. Have children focus on specific questions in their interviews. You might wish to brainstorm questions with the group on chart paper and then decide on the ten most interesting questions. Here are some suggestions:

- When you were young, what toys or games did you play with?
- When you were a child, did you have any pets? What did the pets look like? What were their names?
- Did you ever get sick when you were young? What did you do to get better?
- Were you ever afraid when you were a child?
- When you were young, what was your favorite story?
- What do you remember about school? What did you do there? How did you get there?
- Tell me about any big storms, floods, or snowstorms you experienced when you were a child.
- What special things did you do on vacations when you were young?
- How did you get places when you were a child? What kind of transportation did you use?
- When you were young, who were the most important people in your life?
- When you were a child, where did you live? With whom did you live?

Before children interview family members, try to set up an interview in class with a member of your school staff. Let children take turns asking questions. Then send home written questions with children, and encourage family members to help them record the answers on paper or even on tape. You might ask children to interview the oldest person in their family (or their oldest friend), someone who lives far away, or someone they see all the time. These interviews can be part of an ongoing project that culminates at the end of the year in a recorded family history.

Books for Children

Africa Brothers and Sisters, by Virginia Kroll (Four Winds), tells about the proud and diverse heritage of a young African American boy.

All Kinds of Families, by Norma Klein (Albert Whitman), celebrates the different types of families that exist in our world.

Angel Child, Dragon Child, by Michele Mana Surat (Raintree), tells the story of a young Vietnamese girl and how she adjusts to life, and especially school, in the United States.

Cleversticks, by Bernard Ashley (Crown), a tale of diversity and self-esteem, tells about a Chinese American boy who can't find anything he is really good at, until he realizes that he is the only one who knows how to use chopsticks.

Colors Around Me, by Vivian Church (Afro American), explores differences in African American skin tones.

Cornrows, by Camille Yarbrough (Putnam), is a book which explains the significance to African Americans of braiding hair in rows. The story is told through the eyes of a young girl.

Elaine and the Flying Frog, by Heide Chang (Random House), is the story of a Chinese American girl's adjustment to life in an Iowa school.

Families Are Different, by Nina Pellegrini (Holiday House), was inspired by the author's adopted Korean daughter. Nico is unhappy that she doesn't look like her parents until she realizes that families and their members come in many shapes, sizes, and colors.

People, by Peter Spiers (Doubleday), illustrates the great diversity of the world's population.

The Remembering Box, by Eth Clifford (Morrow), tells of a grandmother's special box filled with objects she uses to share her history with her grandchild.

We Don't Look Like Our Mom and Dad, by Harriet Langsam Sobol (Coward-McCann) discusses cross-cultural adoptions.

Why Am I Different?, by Norma Simon (Albert Whitman), helps children understand differences in physical makeup, personality, and culture, and in the process fosters positive self-image and self-esteem.

Around the World Greetings

Poster Activities

Overview

Background Information

Although all languages have unique words, idioms, and usages, certain communication basics are universal. The *Greetings Poster* includes words and phrases from fourteen languages, chosen to reflect their statistical representation in the United States population (1990 census) and to give children an introduction to a variety of alphabets and syllabaries, which are groups of characters, each of which represents a syllable in a language. In many of these languages, there is more than one form of greeting. For example, in Spanish, *"¡Hola!"* is a more informal greeting than *"Buenos Dias,"* which means "Good day." Also in some languages a specific gesture, such as a bow or shaking hands, often accompanies a greeting.

The *Greetings Poster* and its related activities are designed to set a friendly, inviting tone for multicultural explorations in your classroom. As your children learn verbal (and nonverbal) greetings from around the world, they will become aware that although the words or phrases are different, their purpose is the same. An added benefit of the *Greetings Poster* is that children will become aware that other children around the world learn to read and write, even though the words and the way they are written differ.

Objectives

* To introduce the concept that people all over the world greet each other using different words, phrases, and gestures
* To familiarize children with fourteen of these greetings

Materials

File cards, *Greetings Poster,* copies of the letter on page 35 (one per child), *World Map,* tape or thumbtacks

Explanation of Poster

The chart on the following page is a reference guide to the *Greetings Poster.* In many cases, the pronunciation we have provided for a word or phrase is only one of several that can be used, due to differences in dialects. You may wish to share some of the information in the right-hand column with children.

Language	Greeting	Pronunciation	Other Information
Arabic	اَلسَّلامُ عَلَيْكُمْ	AS-sa-la-mu A-lay-kum	A formal greeting used by Arab Moslems meaning, "Peace be with you." Read from right to left.
Armenian	ԲԱՐԵՒ	BAH-rev	"Good things (to you)," is the actual translation.
Chinese	你 好	ni-HAO	Read from top to bottom; there are many Chinese dialects, this one is widely used.
English	Hello	heh-LO	This is an informal greeting.
German	Guten Tag	GOO-ten tak	"Good day," is the actual translation.
Greek	γειά σου	YA-soo	This greeting literally means, "Be healthy."
Hebrew	שָׁלוֹם	shah-LOM	The translation of this is "Peace." Also used to say "Goodbye." Read from right to left.
Hindi	नमस्ते	na-mas-tay	This salutation is used at all times of the day, for greetings and departures. Read from right to left.
Italian	Ciao	CHOW	This is an informal greeting.
Japanese	こんにちは	kon-ni-chi-wa	Read from top to bottom. This is a general greeting. "Good afternoon" is the actual translation.
Spanish	Hola	OH-lah	This is an informal greeting.
Swahili	Jambo	jahm-BOW	This informal greeting is usually accompanied by a handshake or a slight bow.
Thai	สวัสดี	swad-DEE or sa-wa-sdi	This formal greeting can mean either "hello" or "goodbye." Children would bow to an elder.
Yoruba	Ẹ K'arọ	eKAH-ROH	"Good morning" is the actual translation.

Introduction

Hello Game: Play this game with children during circle time to make children aware that people use different greetings in different situations. Present children with situations similar to the following and let each child have a turn responding with words and/or actions. Try to make the situations as realistic as possible, so children will have an easier time visualizing and then acting out responses. Here are some examples (substitute your students' names).

* *"Tanisha, suppose you're walking down the street and you meet your good friend, Jessica. How would you greet her?"*
* *"Kent, suppose you're walking down the street and you meet your friend, Akkiko, and her new baby brother. How would you greet the baby?"*
* *"Ana, suppose you're walking down the street and you meet your relative who lives far away. How would you greet her?"*
* *"Tyrone, suppose you're walking down the street and you meet the President of the United States. How would you greet him?"*
* *"Raoul, suppose you're walking down the street and you meet a new friend who doesn't speak English. How would you greet him?"*

Special Words to Say Hello: At the end of the day, give one final hypothetical situation, this time from your own experience (if possible) with a relative or friend, using the following as a model:

> *"I was walking down the street and I met my aunt Lupe from Mexico. She said, '¡Hola!'"*

In advance, write a greeting on a file card. Show the card and pronounce the word for children. Explain its significance in your own family history. If you are unable to draw on personal experience for this activity, take an example from children's literature. Read to children a book about another culture, such as one from the *Madeline* series by Ludwig Bemelmans (Random House). Then present this hypothetical situation:

> *"I was walking down the street and I met Madeline. She greeted me and said, 'Bonjour.'"*

Ask children if anyone knows how to say "hello" in another language. Some children may have heard members of their families speak other languages. Propose that the class collect many ways to greet people, using their families as a primary resource. Read children the letter on the facing page and then give each child a copy of the letter with an attached file card to take home.

Hola नमस्ते Jambo שָׁלוֹם Ẹ K'arọ Ciao Hello

Dear Parents,

Your child is learning how people greet each other in many different countries and cultures. We have a poster in our classroom that shows words of greeting in several languages and various alphabets. This poster is introducing your child to the idea that many children all over the world are also learning to read letters and words. At the same time, your child is discovering that other languages and alphabets are different from English. What's more, your child is experiencing the beauty of many languages.

We would like our poster to represent accurately the children in our class and their families. Therefore we are asking you to write a greeting on the attached card in a language other than English, if another language is spoken in your home or if any members of your family speak a second language.

Please return the card by:

_____

When you next visit our classroom, please take a look at our multicultural display. We hope that you will feel very welcome when we greet you in so many languages!

Sincerely,

Working with the Posters

When the file cards with the greetings begin coming in from families, present the *Greetings Poster* to children. Identify the language and alphabet of each word or phrase, and use the pronunciation guides to help you read the words aloud. Depending on the interest and age level of your children, you may wish to tell them some interesting facts about the languages and alphabets presented on the poster. (For instance, Hebrew and Arabic are read from right to left and Chinese and Japanese are read from top to bottom.)

As you introduce a new word, point out places on the *World Map* where it might be spoken. You may wish to make copies of pages 40-44 of this book, cut out the individual words, paste them on index cards, and attach them to appropriate places on the map.

Display the *Greetings Poster* either in your communication center or writing center, or create a Greetings Center. Add to the border of the poster the file cards sent in by parents to create a multicultural bulletin board display that is unique to your classroom. Throughout the year, add cards with greetings from around the world you collect from class visitors, people around the school, and people in the community.

Greetings Center: Use the *Greetings Poster* as the focus of a center in your classroom. Here are some things to include:
* A "Communication Board" on the wall where children can post their greetings
* An in-class mailbox where children can "send" cards to each other
* A cassette player with a tape of people saying "hello" in different voices, accents, and languages. Elicit help from parents and school personnel to create the tape.
* Postcards and greeting cards from far away places, displayed on the Communication Board

Follow-Up Activities

Art

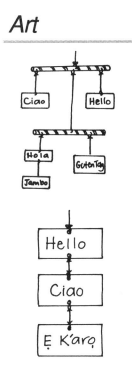

Greetings Mural: Have a wide variety of shades of construction paper available. Let children draw themselves on paper and then cut out the pictures. On mural paper, draw a long, horizontal groundline indicating a sidewalk. Glue the drawings of children on the paper as though they are walking down the sidewalk, greeting each other. Draw a cartoon-style speech bubble next to each child's head. Help children write their favorite greeting in their bubbles. Let children add other details to the mural like trees, houses, and pets. Display the mural in the classroom.

Greetings Mobile: Make copies of the words and phrases on pages 40-44. Have children cut out each word or phrase and glue it onto a file card. Let children decorate the blank side of each card *or* back each card with colored paper or foil. Punch a hole in the middle of the top and bottom of each card. Suspend cards together (using string or yarn) in as shown at the right.

Printed Greetings: Give children rubber stamp letters, available in teacher's supply stores and catalogs. Let children print greetings in English and other languages.

Math

Counting Letters: Have children look at the words on the *Greetings Poster* and count the letters or characters that make up each greeting. In which language does the greeting have the most letters or characters? In which does it have the least?

Greetings Card Games: Make up sets of cards, using the models on pages 40-44. Let children play matching games, such as Go Fish or Old Maid (with "Goodbye" as the Old Maid card), and memory games, such as Concentration.

Science/Nature

Animal Communication: Talk with children about how animals communicate. Have children take turns imitating the sounds of their favorite animals. Let others guess the animal. Discuss whether one type of animal can communicate with another type. Have children pretend to be different animals in the jungle, the forest, or the barnyard. Have them try to communicate with each other. What might they have to communicate to each other? Play tapes of animal sounds. Play a tape of whale or dolphin sounds; scientists have found that these animals communicate with their own "language."

Whole Language

Picture Pal Exchange: Consider starting an exchange with a class of children from another country. Here is an organization that can help.

• *Paintbrush Diplomacy,* 1717 17th Street, San Francisco, CA 94103 (415-255-7478) Germaine Juneau, Director.

This organization arranges exchanges of children's art and letters between schools here and abroad. Not for individuals, only classes of children.

Greetings Stories: Help children create stories that begin when two people (or animals or imaginary beings, such as creatures from Mars) meet and greet each other. Let them write, dictate, or draw pictures to tell their stories. You may wish to bind the stories together with a cover and put this Greetings Book in your library corner.

Language Development

Words from Around the World: Share with children words in our language that are derived from other languages; for example, *candy*—Sanskrit, *tea*—Chinese, *chimpanzee*—West African, *kayak*—Inuit. You may wish to write the words and draw simple illustrations for each one on cards or large chart paper and add this to your multicultural display. Use the *World Map* to help children place the countries of origin for the words.

Lots of Goodbyes: Children might like to learn how "goodbye" is said in different languages: *addio (add-I-oh)*—Italian, *sayonara (sigh-OH-na-ra)*—Japanese, *adios (ah-dee-OHS)*—Spanish, *shalom (sha-LOM)*—Hebrew.

Field Trips

Greetings Around the School: Take a walk around the school with children to collect "hellos" in different languages. Be sure to take file cards and pencils with you. Talk to teachers, staff, and maintenance people, and perhaps visit other classes to build your collection.

Greetings Around Town: Whenever you take field trips, take along a supply of file cards and markers. You never know who you might meet at the supermarket, police station, or library.

Foreign Speakers: Visit a high school language class or college language lab or invite students to visit your class. Students of foreign languages usually will be happy to share their knowledge of other cultures as well as translating words and phrases which interest your children.

Extending the Theme

Social Studies/Art

Writing from Long Ago: The first examples of writing that have been found were created over five thousand years ago in a place called Sumer in the Middle East. Long ago people wrote on wet clay with a pointed tool called a stylus. Let children make clay tablets and write on them with pointed objects. Have children brainstorm different objects they could use to write with.

Natural Inks: Long ago, people all over the world made inks with natural materials they had close at hand. Make natural inks by brewing strong tea or boiling onion skins. Give children feathers with their ends cut on a diagonal to dip into the cooled liquid and use as pens.

Books for Children

Alphabet Art, by Leonard Everett Fisher (MacMillan), gives children examples of thirteen different alphabets and syllabaries.

Jambo Means Hello, by Muriel Feelings (Dial), is an alphabetical introduction to the culture of East Africa.

Amigo Means Friend, by Louise Everett (Troll), demonstrates that language does not have to be a barrier to friendship.

I Hate English, by Ellen Levine (Scholastic), tells the story of a young Chinese girl who struggles with English—and the teacher who helps her learn the language.

Count Your Way Through (Name of Country), by Jim Haskins (Carolrhoda), is a series of twelve books that teaches the numbers one to ten in settings around the world.

Chinese Mother Goose, edited by Robert Wyndham (Philomel), features rhymes along with Chinese script translations.

This Is My House, by Arthur Dorros (Scholastic), shows houses from around the world. The phrase, "This is my house," is featured with each home in the language of the culture.

The Dancer, by Fred Burstein (Bradbury), features words and phrases in English, Spanish, and Japanese.

السَّلامُ عَلَيْكُمْ

Arabic (AS-sa-la-mu A-lay-kum)

ԹԱՐԵՒ

Armenian (BAH-rev)

Hello

English (heh-LO)

Guten Tag

German   (GOO-ten tak)

γειά σου

Greek   (YA-soo)

Hebrew   (Shah-LOM)

Hindi (na-mas-tay)

Ciao

Italian (CHOW)

Hola

Spanish (OH-lah)

Jambo

Swahili   (Jahm-BOW)

สวัสดี

Thai   (Swad-DEE)

Ẹ K'aro

Yoruba   (eKAH-ROH)

Chinese
(Ni-HAO)

Japanese
(kon-ni-chi-wa)

Around the World
from A to Z

Poster Activities

Overview

Background Information

The *A to Z Poster* has been designed to help you weave multicultural themes into your daily routine. The items on the poster represent a wide variety of cultures around the world. They also tie into content areas of interest to young children, such as clothing, food, and transportation. The items can act as springboards, letting children explore a particular multicultural theme. For example, *ibheque* are Zulu beads that carry messages of feeling. These beads can lead to explorations of how beads are used in different cultures, from worry beads in the Middle East to bead gardens in Holland. Also, different expressions of feeling can be explored, from friendship bracelets to greeting cards.

Most of the items on the poster are labeled with the name given to them in the language of the culture they represent. In some cases, however, they are labeled with an English word, either because they fit into the alphabet format or because they are found in several cultures with different names.

We encourage you to introduce the items naturally into your existing curriculum. Here are some suggestions.
• If you use a "Letter of the Week" theme in your classroom, the items can be integrated by their initial letter.
• The items can also fit into common themes, such as transportation, animals, and folktales, often studied as units in early childhood classrooms.
• Some items will fit naturally into center-related activities, such as cooking (baguettes), art (ofrenda pictures), and reading (Anansi).
• Items can be studied because children or parents have an interest in them.

Each lesson begins with background information, objectives, and a list of materials needed to complete the Introduction and Working with the Poster activities. The Introduction activity familiarizes children with the content area associated with the item or to pique their curiosity about the item itself. The *World Map* and the *Greetings Poster* become part of the lesson as children see where in the world the item comes from and how people of that culture greet each other.

The suggested Follow-Up Activities will enable you to integrate the item or the theme into several content areas in your curriculum. Each lesson has one or more book suggestions in the Follow-Up section to teach children more about the culture from which the item comes. Use the photographs and other illustrations in these books as you would use postcards, encouraging children to point out what they see and how it is similar to or different from their own experiences. Use the text of the book for your own information.

In the Extending the Theme section of each lesson, there are book suggestions to extend the lesson theme to other cultures. Books are an excellent way to give children a glimpse of the ways other people live and a positive way to discuss similarities and differences.

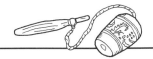

Dear Parents,

In the coming weeks, we will introduce your children to objects, people, and ideas from many cultures around the world. We hope to help children develop an understanding and appreciation for their own traditions and cultural backgrounds as well as those of others. Through this sharing, everyone will be enriched and learn respect for differences.

Please take a moment to review the information at the bottom of this letter. It is a list of the multicultural themes we will explore and specific examples of the items children will learn about. Please use the blank spaces to jot down anything you would be willing to share with the class (either in person or through your child) concerning these themes and items. Thank you for your help.

Sincerely,

- -

NAME _____   CHILD _____

THEMES   POSSIBLE ITEMS TO SHARE

Folktales (examples: Anansi, Raven)   _____

Food (breads, treats, rice dishes)   _____

Folk Art (dream catcher, ofrenda pictures, wycinanki)   _____

Shoes (geta)   _____

Games (hop-round, valero, tiu-ü)   _____

Jewelry (ibheque)   _____

Baskets (kiondo)   _____

Dolls (matroshka dolls)   _____

Hats (non la)   _____

Modes of Transportation (junk, qamutig, elephant)   _____

Musical Instruments   _____
(castanets, shekere, xylophone, `ud, zampoña)

Anything else you would like to share to help   _____
children learn about another culture

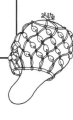

Anansi

Background Information

Anansi (ah-NAHN-see) is a popular hero-trickster in West African folklore. The Anansi stories are part of an oral tradition; they were usually told by storytellers and not written down in books. Anansi can be found in many countries, including Ghana, Liberia, Congo, and Angola. Anansi takes many forms; sometimes he is a spider, sometimes a man–*Kwaku* (Uncle) *Anansi*–and sometimes a spider-man. But he is always crafty and greedy, trying to outwit the creatures of the jungle, people, and sometimes gods.

In some tales, Anansi falls into traps of his own making and outwits himself. These stories contain morals or lessons for life, much like Aesop's fables or many of the Native American folktales. Other tales, like "Anansi and the Pot of Wisdom," explain human traits, natural phenomena (why spiders build their webs in dark corners), or the beginnings of traditions and customs (why people use the hoe for planting).

Storytelling is an important tradition shared by many cultures around the world. Folktales involving spiders are also told by Native Americans and by Tahitians, who believe spiders to be shadows of the gods, never to be harmed.

Objectives

* To introduce the concept that children all over the world listen to stories
* To familiarize children with the oral tradition of storytelling
* To introduce children to the African folk character Anansi

Materials

"Anansi and the Pot of Wisdom" story on page 126, drawing paper, crayons or markers, *A to Z Poster*, black-and-white illustration on page 100, *World Map*, string, tape or thumbtack, *Greetings Poster*, file card or sticky-back note

Introduction

Ask children to name some of the stories they enjoy having read to them. Tell them that sometimes stories are not read from books with pictures. Sometimes instead of seeing printed illustrations, children must use their imaginations to create pictures in their minds. Tell children that you are going to tell them a story about a tricky spider named Anansi, and challenge them to try to see the spider in their minds. Before you begin to tell or read "Anansi and the Pot of Wisdom," be sure that everyone knows that *wisdom* means understanding or knowledge.

After reading, give each child a piece of drawing paper. Have crayons or markers available. Encourage children to draw large pictures of Anansi. Then let each child share her picture of Anansi and describe the spider as she visualized it.

Working with the Posters

Tell children that you are going to show them how another artist drew Anansi. Highlight the picture of the spider on the *A to Z Poster*. Stories about Anansi are often told in the country of Ghana. This artist created her drawing of Anansi based on a spider woven into a piece of Ghanaian cloth. Have children identify the colors they see in the picture on the poster. Then show them the large black-and-white illustration.

Show children Ghana on the *World Map*. Put the picture of Anansi beside the map and attach it to Ghana with string.

Tell children that the main language spoken in Ghana is English, but that many people also speak Twi-Akan. Teach children how to greet each other in Twi-Akan dialect: *"Wo ho te sen,"* (woo hoo tee SEN), and add this greeting to the *Greetings Poster* on a file card or sticky-back note.

Follow-Up Activities

Art: Help children make a web for Anansi by cutting six 1-inch notches into a paper plate. Tape a 36-40-inch long piece of string to the back of the plate. Have children make spider webs by winding the yarn around the plate. Help each child cut out her picture of Anansi and attach it to the end of the string.

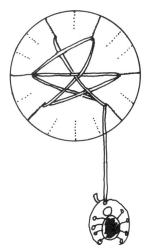

Art/Whole Language: Help children make a mural illustrating another story about Anansi. Select a tale, such as one from *The Adventures of Anansi,* retold by Joyce Cooper Arkhurst (Little, Brown). Tell the story twice and have children help you divide it into scenes as you tell it the second time. Depending on the number of children, give each child or group a scene to draw. Arrange children so that they are working from left to right according to the correct sequence of the story. Let children tell the story, using the pictures on the mural as a guide.

Science: Have children share their own experiences with real spiders in order to learn more about them. For further information, use a book, such as *Spiders,* by Gail Gibbons (Holiday House).

Social Studies: Discuss the pictures in books about life in West Africa today, such as *A Family in Liberia,* by Sally Humphrey (Lerner), to help children learn about these cultures.

Extending the Theme

Greyling, by Jane Yolen (Putnam), is a Scottish folktale about seals who take human form.

Rockabye Crocodile, by Jose Aruego and Arlane Dewey (Greenwillow), is a Filipino fable about a crocodile and her animal baby-sitters.

Baguette

Background Information

A *baguette* (BAHG-ette) is the long slender loaf of bread that is very popular in France. The crust is firm and crunchy, and the bread on the inside is soft and white. This type of bread tends to go stale after a day, so the French buy their baguettes daily.

Baguettes are typically eaten with the midday meal at 2:00 or 3:00 in the afternoon. Many businesses and schools close so that people can go home to eat this large meal and perhaps have a nap. It is not unusual to see children with baguettes in their bicycle baskets on their way home from school.

Baguettes are made with yeast and baked. Similar breads are prepared in many cultures. In Armenia, there is a puffed bread called *peda bread* (pita bread in the United States). In Austria, *kartoffebrot* is made with potatoes. Cubans eat *pan de Cuba de afuera dura. Eshtanore* bread is eaten in Israel. *Semeet* is Egyptian twisted bread. Italians enjoy *pane origano*, made with oregano. In Portugal, *broa* is a coarse bread, eaten with olive oil, and in Sweden, *kryddlimpa* is a spicy rye bread. In China, people steam bread dough to make steam buns.

Objectives

- To introduce the concept that people all over the world eat bread
- To let children see bread in many different shapes and sizes
- To give children experience with the process of shaping and baking bread

Materials

One or two bags of frozen bread dough or a batch of homemade dough, aluminum foil, masking tape, marker, assorted breads or models or pictures of many types of breads, *A to Z Poster,* copies of illustration and recipe on page 101 (one per child), *World Map,* string, tape or thumbtack, *Greetings Poster,* file card or sticky-back note

Introduction

Ask children what kind of bread they like to eat. Then give them hands-on experience with making bread by giving each child a small ball of bread dough on a piece of aluminum foil labeled with the child's name on masking tape. Let children shape their dough however they wish.

Observe the shapes as a group before the bread goes in the oven. Bake according to recipe directions. Then let children observe the baked dough. Have them describe the changes they see. Then let them enjoy their bread at snack time.

Working with the Posters

People all over the world eat some form of bread. Just as there were many different shapes of bread when the children acted as bakers, there are many sizes, shapes, textures, and tastes to breads in different cultures. Show children an assortment of real bread: bagels, challah, hot dog rolls, and so on—pictures, or plastic models of bread.

Then highlight the picture of a baguette on the *A to Z Poster*. Show children the illustration of the bread on the recipe page. Tell children that this bread is eaten every day by many people in France.

Locate France on the *World Map*. Tack the picture of the baguette next to the poster. Connect the picture to France with a string.

If you wish, teach children a French greeting: *"Bonjour"* (BON-zuir), which means "Good day" in English, and add it to the *Greetings Poster*.

Follow-Up Activities

Cooking: Make baguettes with children, using the recipe on page 101, and then send home copies of the recipe so that children can share it with their families.

Science: Do the following experiment to show children why their bread changed shape as it baked.
1. Pour warm water (105-110° F. on a candy thermometer) into two clear glasses.
2. Add a small packet of yeast to one glass. Have children observe how it rises.
3. Put the same amount of yeast in the other glass. Add an equal amount of sugar. Again let children observe how the yeast rises.
4. Have children compare the yeast in the two glasses. The reason that the yeast with the sugar rises so much more is because sugar is food for the yeast. The yeast and the sugar in the bread dough make it rise when it is baked or steamed.

Social Studies: Let children taste different kinds of bread at snack time. If possible, have families share their favorite bread recipes with the class.

Social Studies: Share a book, such as *The Red Balloon*, by Albert Lamorisse (Doubleday), about a child in France.

Extending the Theme

The Sleeping Bread, by Stefan Czernecki and Timothy Rhodes (Hyperion), is a story set in Guatamala about a baker whose bread won't rise.

Tony's Bread, by Tomie DePaola (Putnam), is a tale set in Italy about a baker and his sweet breads.

Bread, Bread, Bread, by Ann Morris (Lothrop, Lee, & Shepard), is a photo essay featuring breads from around the world.

Castanets

Background Information

Castanets (KAS-tan-ets) or *castañuelas* are percussion instruments used in Spanish flamenco dancing. The dancer holds a pair of wooden clappers in each hand by threading the cord that joins the clappers around the thumb and one finger. Castanets are used to keep rhythm with the music and also to sound a long roll.

Instruments similar to castanets are played in many parts of the world. They are called *cai cap ke* in Vietnam, *cascagnettes* in France, *chaharpara* in Roumania, *kayamba* in Kenya, *qaraqib* in North Africa, and *scattagnetti* in Italy.

Flamenco is a dance that originated with the "gypsies" of Southern Spain. It is influenced by music and movement in India, North Africa, and the Near East. Flamenco started as a song and then expanded into a dance and a type of guitar playing.

Objectives

- To introduce the concept that people around the world play rhythm instruments
- To give children the experience of playing an instrument to keep the rhythm while they dance
- To familiarize children with one type of rhythm instrument—castanets

Materials

Percussion instruments, such as rhythm sticks, cymbals, tambourines, musical tapes; *A to Z Poster;* black-and-white illustration on page 102; *World Map;* string; tape or thumbtack; *Greetings Poster*

Introduction

Play a lively musical selection with a strong beat, such as one of the songs on *Multicultural Rhythm Stick Fun* ("Kimbo"), or sing a song or nursery rhyme that children are familiar with. Have children practice keeping the rhythm by clapping their hands. Then give children percussion instruments, or improvise with pairs of tin pie plates and wooden dowels. Again play the music, and have children keep the rhythm with their instruments.

Stop the music and have children lay down their instruments. Start the music again and invite children to get up and dance around, clapping their hands in time to the music. Some children may wish to try moving and playing their instruments at the same time.

Discuss dancing with children. When do children like to dance? What kind of dancing do they enjoy? What are some of their favorite dance songs?

Working with the Posters

Tell children that in many parts of the world people dance and keep the rhythm of the music with instruments. Highlight the castanets on the *A to Z Poster*. Tell children that this pair of clappers is used in Spain to accompany a dance called the flamenco. Show the black-and-white illustration and point out the shape of the wooden clappers and the cord which holds them together.

Find Spain on the *World Map*. Put the picture of the castanets next to the map and attach it to Spain with string.

Tell children that people in Spain speak Spanish. Refer children to the *Greetings Poster* and ask if anyone can remember one way to greet someone in Spanish. ("*¡Hola!*") Ask children if anyone knows any place else in the world where people speak Spanish. Find any country that children mention on the *World Map*.

Follow-Up Activities

Music/Movement: Lead children in a variety of clapping sequences, or let each child have a turn leading while the rest of the group responds. The hand clapping in flamenco is called *palmas*. Another aspect of flamenco dance is the rhythmic sound made by slapping flat feet against the floor. Let children try foot stomping, which is called *golpe* in Spanish.

Art/Music: Help children make their own castanets.

Materials: cardboard strips (about 5 by 1 3/4 inches) or 3-by-5-inch file cards cut in half horizontally; glue; large buttons or soda bottle caps

What to Do:

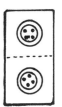

1. Give each child a cardboard strip. Help him place a large dab of glue on each end of the strip. Set a large button into each dab of glue and let dry thoroughly.
2. Help children fold the strips in half so that the buttons are touching.
3. Let children practice tapping the ends together, copying a rhythm, or keeping time to a musical selection.

Social Studies: Share pictures of Spain from a book, such as *Spain (Enchantment of the World Series),* by Esther and Wilbur Cross (Children's Press).

Extending the Theme

Around the World in Dance, by Buzz Glass (Educational Activities), is a recording of folk music from around the world with instructions for folk dances.

Arroz con Leche, selected by Lulu Delacre (Scholastic), features popular songs and rhymes from Latin America.

Dance a Story, Sing a Song, by Marcia Berman and Ann Barlin (Berman and Barlin), is a recording of multicultural songs with suggestions for movements.

Dream catcher

Background Information

Made primarily by the Ojibwe, Oneida, and Sioux peoples, dream catchers are hung above a person's bed to assure good dreams. According to legend, the night air is filled with both good and bad dreams. Dream catchers are made of a loop of willow with a web made of sinew woven inside. The web is created with an opening in the center so that good dreams can pass through the opening and bad dreams will get tangled in the dream catcher. The bad dreams are thought to disappear when the sun shines, much as a spider's web seems to disappear when hit by light at a certain angle. Feathers and beads are often attached to the center to further insure a good night's sleep. Small dream catchers are hung above cradle boards, so that babies have sweet dreams.

Objectives

- To introduce the concept that everyone has dreams—both good and bad
- To explore ways people try to promote good dreams
- To introduce children to a cultural art object, made and used by several Native American nations—the dream catcher

Materials

Sheets of 12-by-18-inch manila drawing paper (one piece per child), markers or crayons, stapler, *A to Z Poster,* copy of page 103, *World Map,* string, tape or thumbtack, *Greetings Poster,* file card or sticky-back note

Introduction

Talk about dreams with children. Ask if anyone would like to share a dream that she remembers. Talk about the difference between good and bad dreams, or "sweet dreams" and nightmares. Encourage each child to tell what she does at night to encourage good dreams. Then give children large pieces of manila paper. Help each child write down her "good dreams" suggestion, and invite the child to draw a picture to go with the writing. Decide ahead of time whether children should illustrate a horizontal or a vertical sheet. When children have finished their drawings, bind the sheets into a Big Book. Staple the pages together, or punch them with three holes, and bind them with metal rings.

Working with the Posters

Read the Big Book with children, and then highlight the dream catcher on the *A to Z Poster.* Tell children that some people think that dream catchers help people have good dreams. Show children the black-and-white illustration. Explain how the dream catcher is supposed to work.

Tell children that dream catchers are part of several Native American traditions. Show children what parts of the United States are the traditional homes of the Sioux (primarily North and South Dakota), Oneida (Wisconsin, New York, and Canada), and Ojibway (Midwest), on the *World Map*. Put the picture on the side of the map and connect it to these areas with string.

Teach children one way people greet each other in the Sioux language: "*Hau*" (HOW). Add this to the *Greetings Poster*.

Follow-Up Activities

Art: Help children make small "sweet dreams" nature pillows. Explain that many people take something special to bed with them to make them feel safe and promote good dreams.

Materials: clean, large men's socks (one per child); sweet-smelling natural materials like herbs, flowers, spices, pine cones or needles; needle; thread

What to Do:

1. Help children collect sweet-smelling items from nature. Dry the herbs and flowers on paper in a dry, airy place, out of the sunlight.
2. Have children mix the natural materials together.
3. Have each child fill a sock with the scented mix.
4. Stitch closed the sock opening.

Children's Literature: Another interesting aspect of the dream catcher is its connection to spiders and their webs. There are Native American legends about spiders who are tricksters. Compare one of these, such as *Ikomi and the Berries,* by Paul Goble (Orchard), with the African stories of Anansi. Discuss with children why they think that people are so intrigued by spiders and their webs.

Social Studies: Share with children information and photos about contemporary Native American cultures using books, such as *Pow Wow,* by June Behrens (Children's Press); *Sacred Harvest,* by Gordon Reguinti (Lerner); *Clambake: A Wampanoag Tradition,* by Russel M. Peters (Lerner); *The Sioux,* by Alice Osinski (Children's Press).

Extending the Theme

Northern Lullaby, by Nancy White Carlson (Philomel), is an Alaskan lullaby illustrated with wonderful, magical, traditional art.

Dreamcatcher, by Audrey Osofsky (Orchard), is the tale of an Ojibway big sister who makes a dream catcher to protect the baby's sleep.

 **E***lephant*

Background Information

Elephants are the largest land animals. There are two main types: Asian or Indian elephants and African elephants. Asian elephants are smaller and have smaller ears. They have a high forehead with two prominent "bumps." Their backs arch up in the middle. Usually only male elephants have tusks. Female elephants of both species are usually a foot and a half shorter than the males and weigh much less. Male elephants are called bulls, female elephants are called cows, and baby elephants are called calves. Asian elephants can live as long as 70 to 80 years.

Wild elephants are caught and trained to do heavy labor in Southern Asia. Such training is possible because elephants are so intelligent.

Wild elephants are an endangered species. All elephants have huge appetites. Since Asian elephants live mostly in forests, they usually eat the leaves of bushes and trees, but they will also eat grass. People are taking the land away that the elephants need to find food. In Africa, elephants are still being killed for their valuable ivory tusks, even though hunting them is illegal.

Objectives

- To have children explore the some of the physical characteristics of Asian elephants
- To introduce the concept that elephants work with people

Materials

Chart paper, chalk, string, tape, *A to Z Poster,* black-and-white illustration on page 104, *World Map,* tape or thumbtack, *Greetings Poster*

Introduction

Ask children if they know what an elephant looks like. Encourage them to describe this animal to you so that you would recognize it on a walk through the jungle. Record descriptive words and phrases on chart paper. One word children will probably use often in their descriptions is "big." Help them explore the actual size of elephants through the following experiences.
- How tall is an elephant? Challenge children to show you how tall they think elephants are by putting a piece of masking tape on the wall at that height. Help children to put tape up higher than they can reach. Use a chair if necessary. Asian elephants can grow to nine feet tall, probably taller than the height of the ceiling in your classroom.

- How long is an elephant? Go out into a long hall with children, and challenge them to show you how long an elephant is by putting string on the floor. Show them the length of an Asian male by stretching 12 feet of string along the floor.

Working with the Posters

Highlight the picture of the Asian elephant on the *A to Z Poster*. Then show the black-and-white illustration. Explain that in India, because elephants are so big and strong, they are used to help people clear forests and do other kinds of hard jobs. Have children think of other jobs that elephants might help with.

Find India on the *World Map*. Put the picture of the elephant on the side of the poster and attach it to India with string. Tell children that this elephant can also be found in other countries in Southeast Asia.

Many languages are spoken in India. English is one of them. Refer children to the *Greetings Poster,* and see if anyone can remember how to greet a friend in Hindi, another language of India. (*"Namaste."*)

Follow-Up Activities

Social Studies: Tell children that elephants are also native to another part of the world—Africa. Together, find Africa on the *World Map*. African elephants are larger than those in Asia. African elephants are not caught and trained to work, as they are in Southeast Asia; they live in the wild all their lives. Let children compare photos or illustrations of both types of elephant.

Science/ Social Studies: Elephants are endangered in both Asia and Africa. Talk about other endangered species. Children might like to make posters to remind people to take special care of animals that face extinction.

Social Studies: Share stories and photographs that will help children understand what life is like in India with books, such as *The Very Special Sari* and *Lost at the Fair*, both by Feroza Mathieson (R & C Black).

Extending the Theme

The Blind Men and the Elephant, retold by Karen Backstein (Scholastic), is a folktale from India.

Llama and the Great Flood, by Ellen Alexander (Harper Collins), is the story of an Andean family saved from a flood by their llama.

My Grandma Lived in Gooligulch, by Graeme Base (Australian Book Source), is a tale with rhythm and repetition that features many animals unique to Australia.

Fry bread

Background Information

Fry bread is one of the most widespread of modern Native American foods. It is served at pow wows, rendezvous, and other large gatherings in many regions as a festive snack; it is also part of everyday cooking in many areas. Though the recipes vary from group to group and from one cook to another, they always call for some kind of flour, baking powder, salt, and water or milk. The dough is patted or rolled into the desired shape—square, round, or triangular, depending on the region—and deep-fried until, golden, puffy, and crisp on the outside. Fry bread is often served with honey or powdered sugar. Plains nations enjoy sweetened chokeberry gravy or sauce with their fry bread. The Ute, who live primarily in Utah and Colorado, use the same dough, but instead of frying it, they cook it over charcoal outdoors or over an open fire. It is often served with roasted meat, fried tomatoes, and green chilies.

People of many cultures enjoy fried breads. Italians make *pizza fritte*. In Spain, people enjoy *churros*. In Mexico, they prepare *buñuelos*.

Objectives

- To introduce the concept that people around the world eat bread prepared in different ways
- To give children experience preparing a fried bread

Materials

Copies of the recipe on page 105 (one per child), unbleached flour, baking powder, salt, warm water or milk, oil or shortening, mixing bowl, spoon, frying pan or electric skillet, *A to Z Poster*, *World Map*, string, thumbtack or tape, *Greetings Poster,* file card or sticky-back note

Introduction

If you have already done the lesson on baguettes, help children recall the different kinds of bread they learned about. Make fry bread in your classroom to introduce children to the idea that bread can be fried as well as baked. Follow the instructions on page 105, letting children do as much of the preliminary work as possible. Make sure that children are not close to the pan as you fry the dough.

Serve the fry bread with jam, powdered sugar, or honey.

Working with the Posters

Tell children that the recipe you prepared comes from a Navajo woman who lives in New Mexico. Highlight the basket of fry bread on the *A to Z Poster*. Ask questions such as, *"Does this fry bread look like the fried dough that you made?"*

Point out the basket. Talk about the colors and designs. Tell children that the Navajo make baskets like this one out of woven fibers. They create different colors with natural dyes made of berries.

The Navajo live primarily in New Mexico, Arizona, and Utah. Find these areas for children on the *World Map*. Put a copy of page 105 next to the map and connect it to the map with string.

Teach children one way that Navajo people greet each other: *"Ya' at' eeh,"* (yah-AHT-ay), and add a card with this phrase to the *Greetings Poster*.

Follow-Up Activities

Cooking: Give children copies of page 105 to take home and share with their families. Ask parents to share any fried dough recipes they might have from other cultures; these might be used either as a cooking experience with children or as a snacktime treat.

Social Studies: Native American peoples from all over the United States eat some form of fry bread. Locate a Native American group in your area, and invite a representative to visit your classroom. Find out if there is a local recipe for fry bread.

Art: Let children "weave" baskets to hold food or other treasures. Give each child a clean berry basket and yarn. Show children how to weave the yarn in and out of the holes.

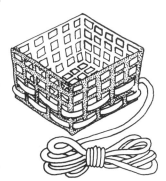

Social Studies: Share with children stories and photographs about the lives of Native Americans in the Southwest, such as *The Navajo* by Alice Osinski (Children's Press), *Pueblo Boy: Growing Up in Two Worlds,* by Marcia Keegan (Cobblehill Books), and *Pueblo Storyteller*, by Diane Hoyt-Goldsmith (Holiday House).

Extending the Theme

Bread, Bread, Bread, by Ann Morris (Lothrop, Lee & Shepard), is a photo essay featuring breads around the world.

Thunder Cake by Patricia Polacco, (Putnam), tells of a grandmother who uses a day of baking to distract her granddaughter from a fearsome thunderstorm.

Geta

Background Information

A *geta* (GAY-ta) is a Japanese sandal with a thick wooden sole, which protects the foot from mud or dirt. The wooden base is held in place by two straps of leather, velvet, or other fabric which pass between the first two toes. Long ago, many people in Japan went barefoot. Today, people still enjoy going barefoot indoors, so they like a shoe that slips on and off easily. Geta are unisex shoes; however, the female model has a flat sole, while male model has a two- to six-inch broad platform. Toddlers in Japan get their first pair of geta when they begin to walk.

Geta are most often worn with *tabi*, a padded white cotton sock. Like a mitten, the tabi has a separate place for the big toe. In wet weather, the geta and tabi are worn with a rubber covering over the front of the foot.

People wear wooden-soled shoes in many cultures. In Africa, they are often carved and brightly painted sandals with leather straps. In Belgium, Holland, and France, people wear wooden-soled clogs to work. They are called *sabots* in France and Belgium and *klompen* in Holland.

Objectives

- To introduce the concept that people all over the world wear foot coverings
- To have children explore the different types of shoes and the reasons why they are worn
- To familiarize children with one special type of shoe—the geta

Materials

An assortment of shoes, *A to Z Poster,* black-and-white illustration on page 106, *World Map,* string, tape or thumbtack, *Greetings Poster*

Introduction

Play the Shoe Detective Game to introduce children to the concept that foot coverings are worn for different reasons. Show children an assortment of shoes worn by people of different ages for different purposes; for example, baby booties, sneakers, work boots, galoshes, high heels, and slippers. Encourage children to play detective and answer the following questions, explaining their reasoning:
- Who would wear this kind of foot covering? How can you tell?
- What might people be doing when they wear this kind of foot covering? How can you tell?
- What type of weather would these shoes be worn in? How can you tell?
- What kind of shoes would you wear in a very cold place? A very warm place?

Discuss with children the idea that the type of foot covering people wear depends on the climate and the type of activity they wear it for.

Working with the Posters

Highlight the picture of the geta on the *A to Z Poster*. Then show children the large illustration of the sandal. Point out the wooden platforms and the fabric straps. Ask some of the same questions about the geta that you asked in the previous activity. Tell children that people of all ages wear geta in Japan.

Locate Japan on the *World Map*. Attach the picture of the geta on the side of the *World Map*. Connect the picture to Japan with string.

Remind children of the Japanese greeting: *"konnichi-wa."* See if anyone can point out the word on the *Greetings Poster*.

Follow-Up Activities

Math: Use shoes for nonstandard measurement. Have each child trace her shoe on oaktag, manila or heavy construction paper, and cut out the tracing. Then have children label this pattern with their name and shoe type. Demonstrate how to use the pattern to measure objects in the room. Divide the class into three groups. Have each child in one group find items the same length as her shoe, children in another group items that are longer, and the third group items that are shorter.

Art: Distribute magazines and catalogs and let children make a shoe collage. Have them cut out pictures of shoes, on people's feet or alone, and paste the pictures on construction paper.

Whole Language: Have each child choose one pair of shoes either from your display, from their collage, or from a magazine and dictate or write a story about the shoes. Who wears the shoes? When do they wear them? Where do they go? What do they do?

Social Studies: If parents have sent in shoes from other cultures, let children be Shoe Detectives to learn about each one. Then create a shoe display.

Social Studies: Give children the flavor of life in Japan today with a book such as *A to Zen,* by Ruth Wells (Picturebook Studios).

Extending the Theme

Not So Fast, Songolo, by Niki Daly (Viking), is the story of a young African boy's trip to the city, where he sees a pair of sneakers he really wants.

A World of Shoes, by Della Rowland (Contemporary Books), describes footwear worn by children in Russia, Holland, Japan, England, and other cultures.

Hop-round

Background Information

Hop-round is a British version of the popular game hopscotch. It is played on a circular pattern drawn on a paved surface.

It is thought that the game was brought to England many centuries ago by Roman soldiers because the pattern of the board closely resembles the wheel of ancient Roman carts. Similar patterns have been found in the ruins of a Roman forum.

To play hop-round, each person throws or rolls five pebbles on the board. The player must hop around the pattern until he reaches a space containing a pebble, which he must pick up without stepping on a line or putting down the other foot. After successfully picking up all five pebbles, the player earns the sum of the numbers in the spaces where the pebbles landed and can claim any space on the board by placing all his pebbles in that space. The next player has to hop over all claimed spaces while picking up her pebbles. The winner is the player who earns a predetermined number of points.

Variations on the game of hopscotch are played all over the world. These games include *pele* in Aruba, *la thunkuna* in Bolivia, *kritz* in Czechoslovakia, *campana* in Italy, and *chilly* in India.

Objectives

- To introduce the idea that children all over the world play similar games
- To introduce a variation on the familiar game of hopscotch—hop-round
- To help children focus on the components of certain games—board, playing pieces, rules

Materials

Chalk, pebbles, chart paper, marker, *A to Z Poster*, black-and-white illustration on page 107, *World Map*, string, tape or thumbtack, *Greetings Poster*.

Introduction

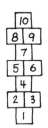

Take the group outside to the playground and draw a simple hopscotch pattern on the ground with chalk. Ask if anyone knows what it is. Have volunteers demonstrate how to play. Talk about the shape of the board. Have children name the numbers. Have each child find a marker, such as a pebble or acorn, to use. If children are unfamiliar with the game, ask an older child to demonstrate, or do it yourself. With children, discuss and then write simple rules on chart paper. Review them several times, so that children can play by themselves.

Working with the Posters

Tell children that games similar to hopscotch are played all around the world. All of these games have a pattern that is drawn on the ground, some form of marker, and rules that involve moving from one part of the board to another in a special way, such as hopping or jumping.

Highlight the picture of hop-round on the *A to Z Poster*. Then show the black-and-white illustration with the gameboard used in England. Have children discuss how this board is different from the one that they use for hopscotch. Ask them what the board reminds them of. Tell children about the history of the game.

Show children England on the *World Map*. Put the picture of hop-round on that side of the map and connect it to England with string.

Ask children if they know what language is spoken in England. Can they think of other countries where English is the most common language?

Follow-Up Activities

Math: Draw a large version of the hop-round pattern on a square piece of oaktag or cardboard to make a math game in the classroom. Have children toss pebbles into the spaces and name the numbers. Children can do simple addition by tossing two pebbles into spaces and adding the numbers. Children can toss a pebble into a space and name the numbers that precede and follow the number their pebble landed on.

Social Studies: Share with children a book about life in England today, such as *A Family in England,* by Jetty St. John (Lerner).

Extending the Theme

The Foxfire Book of Toys and Games, by Linda Garland Page and Hilton Smith (Dutton), is a collection of toys and games from the mountains of Appalachia that came to America by way of Germany, France, and England.

Hopscotch Around the World, by Mary D. Lankford (Morrow Junior Books), teaches sixteen variations on hopscotch from around the world.

Street Rhymes Around the World, edited by Jane Yolen (Wordsong), contains thirty-two street rhymes from seventeen countries, in their original language as well as English.

Ibheque

Background Information

Ibheque (ib-HEE-kay), also known as *ubuhlalo abuhle* ("beautiful beads"), are necklaces woven by the Zulu women of Southern Africa. The narrow beaded band has a square of beadwork in the center which is both an ornament and a form of communication. Sometimes several flaps of beadwork will hang on top of each other and lie like the pages of a book.

The beaded messages can range from declaring love to expressing disappointment. The message is conveyed by the type of bead used, the colors and the patterns woven by the sender. When the messages are very subtle, the color of the pattern and the background must be "read" together to understand the meaning.

Girls will often make a pair of ibheque and give one to a boy and wear the other. This does not mean that they are "going steady," so a boy may wear more than one necklace at a time. Men will often ask their sisters or other female relatives to help them translate the messages.

Beads are used in many ways in different cultures. At one time, beads were used as money. The Dutch make outdoor bead gardens called *tuin kraal*. In many religions, people use strings of beads to help them count prayers and meditations. Many peoples in the Greece and the Middle East use "worry beads" (*called mishbaha* in Lebanese). In most cultures, some form of beads are used for ornamentation as well.

Objectives

- To introduce the concept that there are many ways to show your feelings for other people
- To introduce the idea that people around the world wear beads and give them as gifts
- To introduce a special kind of bead necklace—ibheque

Materials

Assorted colors of construction paper, crayons or markers, scissors, *A to Z Poster*, black-and-white illustration on page 108, *World Map*, string, tape or thumbtack, *Greetings Poster*, file card or sticky-back note

Introduction

Talk about ways to show that you care: words, actions, cards, gifts. Distribute arts and crafts materials and challenge children to make a card without words that illustrates the idea, "I care about you," to a relative, friend, or teacher. Stimulate children's creativity with questions such as the following:

- For whom are you making this card? Why?
- What materials will you use? Why?
- What color or colors will you use? Why?

Working with the Posters

Tell children that people all over the world make things and give presents to express their feelings. Women of the Zulu-speaking peoples of Africa give bead necklaces with important messages of feeling woven into them. Colors, shades of color, and patterns convey these messages. White beads signify love; yellow beads signify wealth; and pink beads signify poverty.

Highlight the ibheque on the *A to Z Poster*. Have children name the colors they see. Show them the large illustration. Talk about the design.

The Zulu-speaking peoples live in the notheastern part of the Republic of South Africa. Put the picture of the ibheque on the side of the *World Map*, and connect it to South Africa with string.

Teach children how people greet each other in the Zulu language: *"Saw'ubona"* (sah-boh-na). Add this to the *Greetings Poster*.

Follow-Up Activities

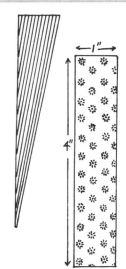

Art: Help children create their own paper beads for stringing.

Materials: assorted paper scraps, including wrapping paper; glue; scissors; pencils; yarn or string; glitter (optional)

What to Do:
1. Have children cut thin strips of paper.
2. Demonstrate how to roll the paper around a pencil and then place a dab of glue on one end of the strip. Allow the glue to dry before slipping the paper bead off the pencil.
3. Beads can be painted or dabbed with glue and then sprinkled with glitter before children string them into necklaces or bracelets.

Social Studies: Share a story about contemporary life in southern Africa; for example, *The Dove,* by Dianne Stewart (Morrow). You might also share some of the photographs from *A Zulu Family,* by Nancy Durrell McKenna (Lerner).

Extending the Theme

Loving, by Ann Morris (Lothrop, Lee & Shepard), is a collection of photographs showing people around the world expressing their emotions.

Nannabah's Friend, by Mary Perrine (Houghton Mifflin), is the story of how a lonely young Navajo girl finds a friend.

Junk

Background Information

The junk is one of the world's oldest sailing ships. The name derives from *chuan*, a Chinese word for boat. Junks can be found today in China, Hong Kong, and Malaysia. This three-masted wooden boat is a double-canoe construction with a blunt, flat bow. Its construction allows for living quarters and/or storage areas inside the bow. Thus the junk is an excellent long-distance cargo ship. Today the junk is used mostly by fishermen.

Junks have special sails that can be raised or lowered easily. On a calm day, the sails are lowered, and the boat is propelled by sailors with long poles. When docking, the junk is sometimes pulled ashore by people wearing tow harnesses.

Boats are an important mode of transportation all over the world. The type of boat found in a given area depends largely on its function and on the materials available to build it. *Umiaks* and *kayaks* are canoes, frequently used for transportation in lands around the Arctic circle. *Gondolas* are the traditional, decorative boats used for transporting passengers through the canals of Venice, Italy. There are many different kinds of sail boats, including the *felucca* in Egypt and the *vinta* in the Philippines.

Objectives

- To let children explore many aspects of one mode of transportation—the boat
- To familiarize children with one type of boat—the junk

Materials

Half-quart or half-pint paper milk cartons (one half carton per child), scrap materials: drinking straws, twigs, play dough, clay, paper or cloth scraps, tongue depressors; string; *A to Z Poster;* black-and-white illustration on page 109; *World Map;* thumbtacks or tape; *Greetings Poster*

Introduction

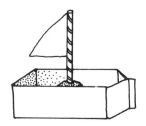

Let children create their own boats to help them explore this important mode of transportation. Tell children to pretend that they are going on a trip and that they need to cross a body of water in a boat. Challenge them to design the boat. Give each child a half-quart or half-pint paper milk carton, cut in half lengthwise to use as a base. Make available a variety of scrap materials for children to use. Ask questions such as the following to stimulate thinking.

- What makes your boat move?
- If this is going to be a long trip, where will you sleep on your boat? Where will you eat? Where will you store your belongings?

- After the trip, what else might you use the boat for?

Have each child explain his boat to the group when it is finished.

Working with the Posters

Discuss the idea that just as children have made different kinds of boats in the classroom, there are many different kinds of boats around the world. Highlight the picture of the junk on the *A to Z Poster*. Then show children the large illustration of this sailing boat. Compare the different features of the junk (bow, sails, etc.) with the boats your children have created.

Junks are used in China and Hong Kong. Locate China on the *World Map*. Put up the picture of the boat on the side of the poster and attach it with string to the area of the world where junks are found.

Refer back to the *Greetings Poster,* and remind children how they might greet children in China. ("*Ni hao.*")

Follow-Up Activities

Social Studies: Using the *World Map*, talk about different trips that could be taken on a boat. Then, put the poster on the floor. (If possible, laminate the poster beforehand.) Also have a large globe available for children's reference. Challenge children to plan trips across bodies of water, plotting their course with the boats they made. Help children identify places on the map, either ones that you have studied or ones they have visited or heard of. You may wish to show children maps of your area that show local bodies of water which children have seen or gone on in a boat.

Science: To find out why boats float, do the following experiment with children, using a lump of plasticene and a tub of water.

1. Have children hypothesize what will happen to the plasticene if you drop it in the water. Do the experiment and discuss the results.
2. Now challenge individuals to mold the plasticene so that it will float. Let several children work with the clay and talk about the results.
3. Help children understand that it is the shape of the clay (boat), not how heavy it is, that determines whether or not it will float.

Social Studies: Help children learn about life in contemporary China with a book, such as *Our Home Is the Sea,* by Riki Levenson (Dutton), which tells about a boy who lives on a houseboat in Hong Kong.

Extending the Theme

Nessa's Fish, by Nancy Luenn (Atheneum), is a story of a young Inuit girl who goes fishing in the Arctic tundra.

Kiondo

Background Information

A *kiondo* (KY-un-dough) is a woven bag used by women in Kenya for shopping in open-air markets. Originally, these colorfully woven baskets made of sisal had no handles and were quite large. In Kenya, kiondos are often made by the women of the Kikuyu tribe and sold to supplement family income that comes primarily from farming. Today kiondos have been adapted to a smaller size with leather straps. They are popular in the United States, where they are often called "Kenya bags."

Baskets are made and used in many cultures. In Malyasia, a *sabah* is a soft and pliable basket. Upper Volta has nesting baskets, akin to *matroshka dolls,* called *mossi lobi.*

Objectives

- To introduce the concept that people all over the world have different ways to carry things from one place to another
- To introduce the concept that the type of carrier used often depends on what is being carried and who is doing the carrying
- To familiarize children with one type of carrier—the kiondo

Materials

A to Z Poster; black-and-white illustration on page 110, *World Map,* string, tape or thumbtack, *Greetings Poster,* file card or sticky-back note

Introduction

Invite children to sit in a circle and play a game of make-believe. Tell children that you are carrying a pretend basket. The basket is filled with apples. Pantomime carrying the heavy basket over to one child. Say: *"I am going to take the apples out of the basket and fill it with feathers."* Ask the child to take the basket filled with feathers from you and carry it to another child. Whenever a child carries the pretend basket to another child, he gets to say what the basket will be filled with and to whom it should be carried (a child who has not yet participated). Tell children that they can imagine anything in the basket, from clouds (that might make you float) to frogs (that might make you jump) to a big rock.

Working with the Posters

Tell children that in Kenya, people carry items in baskets called kiondos.

Highlight the kiondo on the *A to Z Poster*. Show the black-and-white illustration, and tell children that the kiondo is woven of straw.

Find Kenya on the *World Map* and put the picture of the basket next to it. Attach the kiondo to Kenya with string.

People in Kenya and in many parts of East Africa speak Swahili. Refer to the *Greetings Poster* and see if anyone can remember how to greet a friend in Swahili. (*"Jambo."*)

Follow-Up Activities

Social Studies: Have children share any type of bag they brought to school from home. Go around the group and have each child tell what is carried in the bag. Then show children an assortment of carriers. Encourage them to play detective and figure out who might use the carrier, how that person might use it, and what might be carried in it. Let children answer the following questions, and explain their reasoning.

* Who might carry this? How can you tell?
* What might be in it?
* How might this be carried? (Have volunteers demonstrate.)

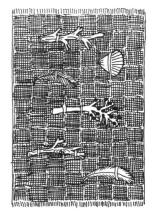

Art: Let children have an experience weaving natural materials using burlap and items children find on a nature walk or which you provide: grasses, feathers, twigs, and so on.

Social Studies: Share with children a book about a child in Kenya, such as *I Am Eyes Ni Macho,* by Leila Ward (Scholastic). Encourage children to talk about what they have in common with the girl in the story. *Kenya Jambo,* by Katherine Perrow and Virginia Overton McLean (Redbird Press), is a book and tape combination introducing life in Kenya through photographs and children's art.

Extending the Theme

Flyaway Girl, by Ann Grifalconi (Little, Brown), is part fantasy and part reality, as a young East African girl helps her mother weave a basket.

Jambo and Other Call and Response Songs and Chants, recorded by Ella Jenkins (Smithsonian/Folkways), offers music inspired by the artist's visit to East Africa.

Masai and I, by Virginia Kroll and Nancy Carpenter (Four Winds), is the story of an African-American child who learns about the tall, proud people of East Africa, the Masai.

Lebkuchen

Background Information

Lebkuchen (leb-KU-shen) are German gingerbread cookies, generally baked and enjoyed at Christmas time. These cookies can be stamped out of very elaborate molds or shaped by hand.   Most recipes call for a combination of exotic spices, including cinnamon, ground cloves, allspice, cardamom, and ginger. Lebkuchen often are baked in the form of pieces for gingerbread houses and frosted for decoration during the holidays.

People all over the world prepare traditional foods for special occasions. In the fall, when Indians celebrate *Diwali*, the Festival of Lights, they eat *ras gulla* (cheese balls dipped in sugar), *jalebi* (fried dough, coated with sugar), and a pudding called *khir*. *Ghuryybeh* is a holiday cookie from Lebanon. The Dutch eat *speculaas* (thin, crispy, spicy brown cookies) and *oliebollen* (doughnuts studded with apples and raisins) on St. Nicholas Eve (December 5). Traditional Christmas foods include *panettone*, a cake in Italy, and *tembleque*, a sweet coconut pudding in the Caribbean and Puerto Rico.

Objectives

* To introduce the concept that people enjoy treats at special times around the world
* To familiarize children with one special treat—lebkuchen, German cookies, enjoyed at Christmas

Materials

Chart paper, markers, *A to Z Poster,* copies of the recipe on page 111 (one per child), spices from recipe, *World Map,* string, tape or thumbtack, *Greetings Poster*

Introduction

My name	My treat is	Special time I eat it

Explore with children the concept of special treats for special occasions. Introduce this activity by asking questions, such as:
* What do you think of when I say 'treat'?
* Who can name some treats you like to eat?

Some treats are eaten at special times. Encourage children to think of special times other than holidays when they eat treats; for example, hot chocolate on snowy days, cotton candy at a fair, or corn on the cob at a family picnic. Make an experience chart to record children's responses.

Working with the Posters

Explain to children that just as they enjoy treats at special times, many children in Germany enjoy special cookies, lebkuchen, at Christmas time. Highlight the picture of the lebkuchen on the *A to Z Poster*. Then show children the larger illustration of the cookies and the recipe. Discuss the recipe. Read the ingredients. If possible, have the spices available for children to smell. Give each child a recipe page to take home and share with her family.

Since lebkuchen are made in Germany, locate this country on the *World Map*. Attach the picture of the cookies on the side of the poster. Put a string from the picture to Germany.

If you have already introduced the *Greetings Poster*, remind children of the German greeting. *("Guten tag.")* Help children point out the phrase on the poster.

Follow-Up Activities

Cooking: Make lebkuchen with children, following the recipe on page 111 or using any simple gingerbread cookie recipe.

Children's Literature/Art: Read a version of the fairy tale, "Hansel and Gretel," a traditional tale from Germany. Then help children make their own simple gingerbread houses. (These are not the edible kind.)

Materials: 1-pint milk cartons, graham crackers, 3 eggs, 1 lb. confectioner's sugar, lemon juice, decorations like raisins, nuts, candies.

What to Do:
1. Make royal frosting by beating 3 egg whites to a frothy foam and adding confectioner's sugar and a few drops of lemon juice.
2. Let children attach graham crackers to milk cartons with frosting.
3. Have children frost crackers and trim with treats.

Social Studies: You might use the chart from the previous page to organize a special treat snack once a month or have a special treat day for which parents are encouraged to contribute traditional special foods for everyone to enjoy.

Social Studies: Share with children photographs of Germany today in books such as *West Germany,* by Barbara Einhorn (Bookwright Press).

Extending the Theme

Matzoh Mouse, by Lauren L. Wohl (Harper Collins), tells of a Jewish girl who nibbles at the chocolate-covered matzoh until there are none left for the Seder.
Yin's Special Thanksgiving by P. Dolgin (January Productions) is the story of Yin's first Thanksgiving in America, when she shares her favorite Vietnamese foods with friends.

Matroshka dolls

Background Information

Matroshka (mah-truesh-kah) dolls are Russian nesting figures. Hand-crafted and painted, they are known around the world as examples of Russian folk art. Nests of 8 and 24 dolls are the most popular; there are sets that contain 50 dolls.

Matroshka dolls are available in a wide variety of personalities and folk costumes. One set may depict the members of a family, while another may show one person at different ages. The most popular matroshka doll is the Semenova version of the peasant woman holding a bouquet of flowers. It is a symbol of renewal, and of Russia itself.

Daruma dolls are roly poly figures that are popular in Japan. The *akuaba* doll from West Africa is a carved wooden figure with an interesting shape. The *saget man* is a figure from Egypt that plays tiny cymbals.

Objectives

- To introduce the concept that people all over the world play with dolls
- To familiarize children with one special type of doll, matroshka dolls
- To explore the concept of graduated size through nesting objects

Materials

Paper, pencils, markers, crayons, *A to Z Poster*, black-and-white illustration on page 112, *World Map,* string, tape or thumbtack, *Greetings Poster,* file card or sticky-back note

Introduction

Give children paper, crayons, pencils, and markers. Have children pretend to be toy makers. Tell them their job is to design a special doll or figure that children would enjoy. Ask questions to stimulate their thinking, such as:
- What will your doll or figure be called?
- What will it be wearing?
- How will children play with it?

Let children share their creations with the group. Tell children that just as they have created many different kinds of dolls and figures, there is a wide variety of dolls around the world.

Working with the Posters

Highlight the picture of the matroshka dolls on the *A to Z Poster*. Then show children the black-and-white illustration. Point out that the dolls in the picture are different sizes. Have one child point to the largest doll, another to the smallest one. Ask children what is special about these dolls. If possible, have an actual set of matroshka dolls to help illustrate the nesting concept. If you do not have the dolls, show children a set of nesting containers, such as measuring cups.

Attach the picture of the matroshka dolls on the side of the *World Map*. Put a string from the picture to Russia. If you wish, teach children a Russian greeting, *"Privet,"* (Priv-YET) and add it to the *Greetings Poster*.

Привет

Follow-Up Activities

Children's Literature/Art: Show children illustrations in a book with Russian folktales, such as *The Turnip,* by Pier Morgan (Philomel). Have them compare the clothing in the illustrations with that of the matroshka dolls (head scarf, colorful patterned fabrics). Help children make paper-cup nesting dolls.

Materials: flat-bottom paper cups of three different sizes, such as 5 oz, 7 oz, 12 oz; construction paper cut into 2-inch paper circles; scissors; fabric scraps; assorted scraps for decoration: sequins, yarn, paper doilies, and so on; marking pens or crayons; glue; (optional wooden ice cream spoon)

What to Do:

1. Give each child one cup in each of the three sizes.
2. Have children turn the cups upside down. On each one, have them glue fabric for scarves and/or other clothing, decorating with assorted scraps.
3. Give each child three paper circles. Have children draw faces for each of their dolls and glue in place.
4. Optional: Have each child decorate a wooden ice cream spoon as the smallest doll, and put it under the smallest cup.

Social Studies: Use the photographs in books, such as *USSR,* edited by Susan Taylor-Boyd, et al. (Gareth Stevens), to give children a picture of everyday life in Russia and other newly independent states.

Extending the Theme

Amoko and the Efua Bear, by Sonia Apiah (Macmillan), is the story of a small girl in Africa who experiences great sorrow when a beloved toy is left out in the rain.

The Chalk Doll, by Charlote Pomerantz (J. B. Lippincott), tells of a Jamaican mother who shares her story of childhood play and the importance of imagination.

The Wooden Doll, by Susan Bonners (Lothrop, Lee & Shepard), follows a Polish child who becomes interested in her grandmother's doll.

Non la

Background Information

A *non la* (nohn la) is a wide, cone-shaped straw hat worn by Vietnamese farmers as they work in the rice fields. Since this style of hat gives protection from the strong sun, it is worn by many other Vietnamese as well.

Similar hats are worn in other parts of Asia, including the *nung fu mao* in China and the *chapil* in Indonesia. In the Philippines, people often wear an "umbrella hat."

People of many cultures wear distinctive hats. The *chullo* is a close-fitting woolen cap worn in Peru. In the Balkans and North Africa, many people wear a *fez*, a cone-shaped hat with a flat top and a tassel. The *berritta* of Italy and the *beret*, worn in France, are similar in style.

Objectives

- To introduce the concept that people all over the world wear hats
- To let children examine different types of hats and the reasons for which they are worn
- To introduce children to one kind of hat—the non la, worn in Vietnam

Materials

A variety of hats, *A to Z Poster,* black-and-white illustration on page 113, *World Map,* string, tape or thumbtack, *Greetings Poster,* file card or sticky-back note

Introduction

Share with children a variety of hats worn by people of different ages for different reasons: baby bonnet, rain hat, ski cap, bike helmet, baseball cap, hard hat, sun visor, and so on. Encourage children to play detective and find out who wears these hats and why. Ask the following questions.
- Who might wear this hat? How can you tell?
- What might the person be doing when he or she wears this hat?
  How can you tell?
- In what kind of weather might a person wear this hat? How can you tell?
- What kind of hat might you wear if you lived in a very cold place? A very hot, sunny place? A very rainy place?

Discuss with children the concept that the type of hat people wear depends on the climate and the type of activity they wear it for. Encourage children to discuss hats that they like to wear and when they like to wear them.

Working with the Posters

Highlight the picture of the non la on the *A to Z Poster*. Then show children the black-and-white illustration of the hat. Tell them that non la are made of woven straw. Ask some of the same questions about this hat that you did about the ones in the introductory activity. Tell children that non la are worn by men, women, and children in Vietnam.

With children, locate Vietnam in Southeast Asia on the *World Map*. Put the picture of the non la next to the map and connect it to Vietnam with string.

Tell children that one way that people greet each other in Vietnam is by saying: *"Chao ban"* (chow-bahn). Add this phrase to the *Greetings Poster*.

Follow-Up Activities

Art: Help children make their own wide-brimmed hats.

Materials: white glue; brush; two sheets of newspaper (22 inches square) per hat; masking tape; newsprint or gift wrap paper; scissors; assorted decorations: ribbons, flowers, feathers, and/or tempera paint and brushes

What to Do:

1. Help each child brush glue all over one side of a sheet of newspaper. Do not saturate with glue. Help the child place a second sheet of paper on top and smooth all over.
2. Place newspaper sheets on top of the child's head and mold paper around the crown of the head. (Note: be sure that children's eyes are not covered.)

3. Wrap long pieces of masking tape around the hat shape while it is still on the child's head in order to create a hat band which will hold the shape of the hat.
4. Carefully remove the hat from the child's head and let it dry overnight. Leave the masking tape in place.

5. The next day, help each child trim her brim to desired shape. Then let them paint or add decorations to their hats.

Social Studies: If possible, show pictures of other head coverings worn in hot, sunny climates. Show children examples of turbans, worn in both African and Asian countries, and the *kaffiyeh*, worn by some Arab males. Give children pieces of cloth and let them experiment with making head coverings.

Social Studies: Share with children information and pictures about life in Vietnam through books such as *Tuan,* by Eva Boholm-Olsson (R & S Books.)

Extending the Theme

Hats, Hats, Hats, by Ann Morris (Lothrop, Lee & Shepard), explores hats around the world through wonderful photographs.

Ofrenda pictures

Background Information

Ofrenda (OH-fren-dah) pictures are made with yarn by the Huichol Indians of West-Central Mexico. These folk pictures range in size from inches to several feet in area. Themes include scenes from Huichol history, village life, and nature. Ofrenda artists are traditionally men. The pictures are created by pressing yarn into beeswax which has been warmed and spread onto a board. Figures are outlined and filled in first and then the background is completed by following the contours of the figures which define the space. A border of several colors edges the paintings. The figures are usually stylized in form. Bright colors are used.

The word *ofrenda* means offering, and if the artist uses a wood backing and rounded corners, these pictures have a religious significance. Otherwise they are considered folk art.

Artists from other cultures create pictures with a wide variety of materials. Native American artists in the Southwest use colored sand to create religious paintings. In Poland, artists use cut paper to create *wycinanki* (see page 92). Pictures called *mosaics,* made with small tiles, are popular in the Middle East.

Objectives

- To introduce the concept that people all over the world create art work using different media and techniques
- To familiarize children with a special genre of folk art—ofrenda pictures
- To give children experience with a particular technique—creating lines, shapes, and designs with yarn

Materials

Flannelboard, 10-to 12-inch piece of colored yarn, assorted lengths of yarn, *A to Z Poster,* black-and-white illustration on page 114, *World Map,* string, tape or thumbtack, *Greetings Poster*

Introduction

Ask children to think of ways to make lines when they are creating a picture. Answers may include markers, glue, paint, chalk, and so on.

Tell children that you are going to show them another way to create lines—by using yarn. Display a flannelboard. (This can be as simple as a piece of felt glued to cardboard.) Using a long piece of colored yarn, create a circle on the board. Ask children to guess the shape. Then let children play a game making shapes for others. Then make a circle again and have children experiment with using yarn to fill in the circle.

Working with the Posters

Highlight the representation of the ofrenda picture on the *A to Z Poster*. Tell children that artists use yarn to create this type of picture. Talk about the colors, and then show the black-and white-illustration and discuss the shape created. Ask children to notice what "kinds of lines" the artist used to create the bird.

Tell children that this type of art is called an ofrenda picture and is done by the Huichol Indians of Mexico. With children, find Mexico on the *World Map*. Put the illustration on the side of the map and connect it to Mexico with string. Review with children other information you may have learned about Mexico.

Look at the *Greetings Poster,* and remind children of how people might greet each other in Mexico. (*"¡Hola!"*)

Follow-Up Activities

Art: Help children make their own ofrenda pictures.

Materials: 8-inch, square pieces of oak tag, white glue in cups, cotton swabs or craft sticks, pencils, bright-colored yarn in a variety of lengths, scissors

What to Do:
1. Demonstrate the entire process (Steps 2-6) before children begin to work.
2. Have children draw the outline of their chosen shape as large as possible with a pencil on an oaktag square.
3. Help children trace over their outlines with glue, using a cotton swab or a craft stick.
4. Help children place yarn over glue. Let them use one long piece or several short ones.
5. Let children spread glue inside the shape.
6. Have children fill in their shapes with yarn.

Math: Make the flannelboard and yarn available in the Math Center along with shape cards for children to try to duplicate on the board.

Social Studies: Help children learn more about Mexico with books such as *The Little Painter of Sabana Grande*, by Patricia Maloney Markum (Bradbury).

Extending the Theme

The Legend of Indian Paintbrush, by Tomie dePaola (Putnam), is the story of a boy who captures the colors of the sunset with a magic paintbrush.

A Young Painter, by Zheng Zhou and Alice Low (Scholastic), is the story of a young artist who created her first watercolor at age three and went on to become a very famous artist in China.

Palay

Background Information

Palay (PAH-lay) is one way to say *rice* in the Philippines. Rice is the main crop of the Philippines because of the tropical climate, abundant rainfall, and fertile soil there. The Philippines are famous for "terrace farming" on the slopes of hills and mountains with an elaborate system for bringing water to the crops.

Filipinos eat palay in many ways. They often eat rice as a main meal with a sauce and chicken or pork. Filipinos enjoy a thick, milky rice gruel called *lugao* as an afternoon snack or *merienda*. They also prepare a sweet, sticky mush of rice mixed with chocolate, called *tsampurada*. Filipinos even make medicine from the hull of burned rice.

Rice is prepared and eaten in many ways around the world. In China, rice is eaten with shrimp, chicken, and vegetables. The Japanese often add soy sauce to their rice, and the Mexicans sometimes add *mole* sauce, a kind of chocolate sauce, to their rice. Many Spaniards enjoy a dish of rice with chicken, sausage, and seafood, called *paella*. The Dutch have a special meal of small dishes made with rice, which they adapted from the Indonesians, called *rijsttafel*. In India, people use basmati rice, which has a special flavor, to make *biryani*, a dish with vegetables, raisins, and nuts. Many Italians enjoy *risotto*, a creamy rice dish that can be prepared in several ways.

Objectives

- To introduce the concept that people all over the world eat some of the same types of food
- To familiarize children with one such food—rice
- To familiarize children with many ways to prepare and eat rice

Materials

Rice cereal; rice cakes; rice dish mixes; different varieties of uncooked and cooked rice: white, brown, wild, basmati; chart paper; marker; *A to Z Poster;* copies of the recipe on page 115 (one per child); *World Map;* string; tape or thumbtack; *Greetings Poster;* file card or sticky-back note

Introduction

Ask children how many of them have had rice to eat. How do they like to eat rice? Ask children to describe their favorite rice dish. What does it look like? How does it taste? Is it hot or cold? Is there a sauce? Is the rice prepared alone or is it mixed with other foods? On a piece of chart paper, record children's answers. Display the rice products and identify them along with several others.

Working with the Posters

Highlight the bowl of palay on the *A to Z Poster*. Tell children that this is a dish of rice from the Philippines, a country where almost everyone eats rice every day. The dish is called a *palay yok*.

Give each child a copy of page 115, and read the recipe with children. Tell them that this is one way that people in the Philippines prepare rice.

Show children the Philippines on the *World Map*. Put the large illustration on the side of the map, and attach it to the Philippines with string.

Tell children that one way people greet each other in the Philippines is by saying: *"kamusta ka"* (kah-MUS-tah kah). Add this phrase to the *Greetings Poster*.

Follow-Up Activities

Social Studies/Cooking: Have children take the recipe sheet home and with their families add a recipe for "My Favorite Way to Eat Rice" to the back of the sheet and return it to school. Collect the recipes and create a *Class Rice Cookbook*.

Social Studies: In different parts of the world, people eat rice with different utensils. Introduce chopsticks to children.

Materials: wooden chopsticks, 2 large rubber bands, construction paper

What to Do:
1. Cut an 8 1/2-by-1-inch strip of paper. Accordion fold the paper.
2. Place the folded paper in between the chopsticks three inches from the top.
3. Secure by wrapping one rubber band tightly around the paper and the chop sticks. (See Diagram A)
4. Wrap the second rubber band around the paper and the first rubber band in between the chopsticks. (See Diagram B) Now children can pick up items by squeezing the sticks together.

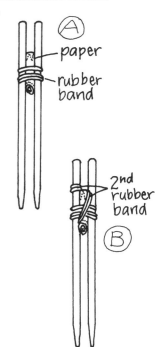

Social Studies: Help children learn more about life in the Philippines, using information and pictures from books such as *Philippines* (*Children of the World Series*), edited by Rhoda Sherwood and Mary Lee Knowlton (Mark J. Sacher).

Extending the Theme

Everybody Cooks Rice, by Norah Dooley (Carolrhoda Books), is the story of a young girl who learns that everyone in her multicultural neighborhood cooks different rice dishes.

Funny Little Woman, by Arlene Mosel (Dutton), is a Japanese folk tale about a little old woman who outwits ogres with a magic rice paddle.

Qamutig

Background Information

The Inuit of the Central Canadian Arctic use a *qamutig* (key-mu-TREK), a special kind of sled, to transport people, equipment, and food across the ice and snow that cover their land all year long. The sled's runners are made of wood (whenever possible) or slabs of ice and frozen fish inside animal skins. The runners are coated with a mixture of moss and snow glazed with ice to insure smooth gliding over the frozen ground. The runners are attached to the frame's crossbars with with sealskin sinew, which is very flexible, thus preventing the qamutig from breaking apart. The crossbars are made of wood or caribou ribs.

In the past, the qamutig was pulled by a team of dogs arranged in a fan shape, instead of a line in front of the sled. This wider formation was possible because there are so few trees in the Arctic landscape. Today, sleds are usually made of wood and are pulled by a snowmobile. In parts of Alaska, children race dog sleds.

Objectives

- To introduce the concept that people all over the world use different forms of transportation, depending on climate and terrain
- To familiarize children with one special type of transportation—the qamutig

Materials

Chart paper; marker; examples or pictures of skis, skates, sleds; *A to Z Poster;* black-and-white illustration on page 116; *World Map;* string; tape or thumbtack; *Greetings Poster;* file card or sticky-back note

Introduction

If possible, take a walk with children outside the school where they can observe several modes of transportation. When you return, make an experience chart listing all the different kinds of vehicles children observed (bikes, cars, trucks, trikes, roller skates, and so on.)

Now ask children to think about or imagine a place where there is ice and snow covering the ground all the time. How might they go from place to place? (Skis and skates are possible answers.) What if they had to move something from one place to another that was too heavy to carry? (Sleds would be useful for transporting cargo.) You may need to help many children understand that they would need different kinds of transportation from what they have at home if they were to live in a place where everything was frozen.

Working with the Posters

If possible, show real examples or pictures of skis, sleds, and skates. Emphasize how each is built to travel over ice and/or snow. Highlight the picture of the qamutig on the *A to Z Poster*. Then show children the black-and-white illustration of the sled. Have children compare the construction of the qamutig with that of the other cold weather apparatus. Tell children that these sleds are used for transporting people and things in the land near the North Pole.

Qamutigs are used in the Arctic region of Canada. Locate this area on the *World Map*. If possible, show children on a globe how close this area is to the North Pole. Attach the picture of the qamutig on the side of the *World Map*. Put a string from the picture to Northern Canada.

The people who use qamutigs are called Inuit. They use many things that are special, because the place where they live is so cold.

Tell children that the Inuit people sometimes welcome each other by saying *"Paglagikpiñ."* (Pahg-lah-gik-peen) Add this word to the *Greetings Poster*.

Follow-Up Activities

Science/Social Studies: Read nonfiction books about life in the frozen North, such as *Eskimo Boy* by Russ Kendall (Scholastic). Talk about the adaptations people make in their homes, food, clothing, work, and play for life in very cold climates.

Art: Have children make "snow goggles." (*Ijjait* in Inuit) Goggles like these are used in the far North to protect peoples' eyes from the glare of the snow.

Materials: 3-by-5-inch file cards, hole puncher, pipe cleaners, scissors
What to Do:
1. Demonstrate and then help children each fold a file card horizontally and cut along the middle of the fold, creating a slit when the card is unfolded.
2. Have children punch holes in the center of both ends of the card.
3. Let children attach pipe cleaners by bending one end through the hole. Have them fit the other end over the ears to hold the goggles on their eyes.
4. Let children wear glasses outside in the sun, if possible on a snowy day. If this is not possible, put a white sheet of paper in sunshine to let children see the strength of the sun's reflection on white.

Extending the Theme

This Is the Way We Go to School, by Edith Bauer (Scholastic), features all the ways children travel to school around the world.

On the Go, by Ann Morris (Lothrop, Lee & Shepard), tells about transportation around the world through stunning photographs.

Raven

Background Information

Raven is an important figure in the mythology of the Northwest Pacific Coast Indian groups, including the Haida, the Tlinget, and the Kwakiutl peoples. Raven is known as a hero-trickster in bird form, but he has many human characteristics, including greed and a voracious appetite. Raven transforms himself into living things as well as inanimate objects during his adventures.

Raven tales often include a lesson or moral, much like those about Anansi, the spider, in West Africa. Raven is also important in a creation myth. This story says that Raven created a vine on which a pea pod grew and that man emerged from the pea pod. Then Raven made other animals and finally woman from clay taken from a creek.

The peoples of the Northwest Coast have lived in the same area for approximately 9,000 years. The Raven stories as well as other mythological tales have been passed from generation to generation by word of mouth. Since the art in this ancient culture is closely linked with the spiritual and ancestral roots of the people, Raven is often represented in totem poles, button blankets, masks, and other works of art.

Tricksters are popular in the folklore of many cultures, including *Ma'ii*, the Navajo coyote; *Br'er Rabbit* in African-American tales; and *Badger* in Japan.

Objectives

* To introduce children to a popular Northwest Coast folklore figure—Raven
* To familiarize children with the tradition of story telling

Materials

"How Raven Stole the Sun" story on page 127, *A to Z Poster,* black-and-white illustration on page 117, *World Map,* string, tape or thumbtack, *Greetings Poster,* file card or sticky-back note

Introduction

Tell children that sometimes stories are told and not read in books, so there are no pictures to show how characters look. Listeners must imagine pictures in their minds. Tell children the story, "How Raven Stole the Sun," to give them experience with the oral tradition. Then ask questions to help them recall the story.
* Why did Raven want to steal the sun?
* Where did the sky chief hide the sun?
* What did Raven change into to fool the chief's daughter?
* How did Raven carry the sun back to Earth?

Working with the Posters

Tell children that the story you told came from a culture on the Northwest Coast of North America. This story was passed down from generation to generation by storytellers, but also through the artwork of the culture.

Highlight Raven on the *A to Z Poster*. Then show children the black-and-white illustration. Explain that this picture is based on a carving done by a contemporary Haida artist, showing Raven with the sun in its beak.

Show children the area on the *World Map*, inhabited by the groups of the Northwest Coast. (Alaska through British Columbia to Washington State) Put the picture of Raven on the side of the map, and connect it to this area with string.

Tell children that the Raven stories are told by several groups, but this particular story is from the Haida people. Teach children a Haida greeting: *"Dang gwaa 'laa"* (DUNG gwa la), and add this to the *Greetings Poster*.

Follow-Up Activities

Whole Language: Raven could transform himself into anything. Ask questions, such as, *"What if Raven came to your school? What would he be disguised as? What would he do?"* Let children help you create a new Raven story. Write their ideas on chart paper. Then let children help you sequence the ideas and create a story. Let each child draw an illustration for the story.

Art: According to the ancient stories of the Northwest, long ago, animals shed their feathers, fur, and scales to become people, starting the first human families or clans. Each large family has a crest that represents their special animal. These crests appear on many of their possessions. Give children paper plates and make available art and collage materials. Let each child choose an animal and create an individual crest. Display the crests, taped vertically to a long narrow box or on a bulletin board to simulate a totem pole.

Art: What color would Raven be if his feathers hadn't been scorched by the sun? Challenge children to draw pictures of what Raven looked like before he carried away the sun.

Social Studies: Help children learn more about life in the Northwest with a book such as *Children, Families, and the Sea,* by Sarah and Peter Dixon (Cypress).

Extending the Theme

Toad Is the Uncle of Heaven, by Jeanne M. Lee (Henry Holt), is a Vietnamese folktale in which a toad brings water to the world.

Elinda Who Danced in the Sky, by Lynn Moroney (Children's Book Press), is an Estonian folktale that tells how the Milky Way came to be.

Shekere

Background Information

A *shekere* (shay-ker-AY) is the Swahili name for a shaker or rattle, used in many African cultures. The same instrument has different names in different countries, including *aqbe* in Nigeria and *lilolo* in the Congo. Shekeres are most often used to play a repetitive rhythm along with drums and other percussion instruments. Shekeres are made of dried gourds with a net of beads or small bones attached to the outside. These gourds are sometimes carved or painted for decoration.

In many cultures, people make shakers from natural materials. The Chinese use a rattle made from bamboo, threaded on the outside with small coins. In Kenya, they use a woven cord rattle called a *sisal*. People in Iran play a *quashig*, which is a spoon-shaped, hollow wooden rattle filled with pellets. Some rattles are made of animal shells, leather, and ivory.

Other musical instruments are made of gourds. The *guiro,* popular in Puerto Rico and Mexico, is struck and scraped with a stick to make sounds. The *vina* is an Indian lute made from two gourds.

Objectives

* To introduce the concept that people all over the world use rattles as musical instruments
* To familiarize children with one special type of rattle—the shekere
* To have children experience the process of making a rattle

Materials

Paper cups, seeds, pebbles, buttons, beads, and other noisemaking fills; strong tape, such as electrical duct tape; markers, crayons, or collage materials; *A to Z Poster;* black-and-white illustration on page 118; variety of gourds; *World Map;* string; tape or thumbtack; *Greetings Poster;* file card or sticky-back note

Introduction

Help children make and play their own shakers to introduce them to the concept of rattles. If possible, display some shakers for children. Tell them that most rattles are containers filled with "noise makers."

What to Do:

1. Give each child two paper cups of the same size. Have each child fill one cup part way with noise makers she has found outside (pebbles, seeds) or in the classroom (old buttons, beads).
2. Help children turn the other cup upside down and place it on top of the first cup, rim to rim. Seal the cups together by wrapping tape around the rims.

3. Let children decorate their rattles with crayons, markers, or collage materials. Have children compare the sounds of their rattles. Talk about why different rattles make different sounds.

Working with the Posters

Just as there are different-sounding rattles in the classroom, there are many different-sounding and different-looking shakers around the world. Highlight the picture of the shekere on the *A to Z Poster*. Then show children the large illustration of the shaker. Tell children that this shaker is made of a dried gourd. If possible, have a variety of gourds in different sizes, shapes, and colors for children to handle. Point out the net of beads on the outside of the gourd. These beads are the noisemakers on this type of shaker.

One place that shekeres are used is Nigeria. Locate this West Central African country on the *World Map*. Attach the picture of the shekere on the side of the poster. Put a string from the picture to Nigeria.

Many people in Nigeria speak Yoruba. See if anyone can remember the Yoruba greeting: *"E K'aro,"* which appears on the *Greetings Poster*.

Follow-Up Activities

Art: To make their rattles more like shekeres, have children cut up plastic straws and string them on yarn. Use a piece of tape at the end of the yarn to make stringing easier. Have them wind the yarn around the rattle. Tape it at top and bottom.

Music: After you demonstrate, have each child take a turn as leader and use the rattle she made to create a simple rhythm. Have other children copy the rhythm. Let children follow the rhythms on African recordings.

Social Studies: Create a class exhibit of rattles, from baby rattles to pictures of rattlesnakes.

Science: Dry out a few different kinds of gourds, and see if they will become rattles when they are hollow and their seeds shake.

Social Studies: Share information and pictures of Nigeria with children using books such as *A Family in Nigeria,* by Carol Barker (Lerner).

Extending the Theme

Caribbean Carnival, Songs of the West Indies, by Irving Burgie (Tambourine Books), is a lively collection of songs inspired by African music.

African Rhythms and Instruments,Vols. 1, 2, 3, (World Music Press), includes representative selections from 19 African countries.

Tiu-ü

Background Information

Tiu-ü (Tee-ew-you), a simple game from China, combines playing pieces very similar to our dominoes and rules similar to the card game, Go Fish. It is played with two sets of Chinese dominoes. These are either ivory, bone, or wood and are longer than Western dominoes. The spots are incised: the one and four spots are marked in red, the others in white, except for the double-six tile which is half red and half white.

Tiu-ü is played by two or three players with two sets of 32 tiles. There are simple instructions on page 119.

Tjak-ma-tcho-ki is a Korean game, similar to dominoes. Domino games are played widely in many countries around the world. *The Block Game* is popular in Panama. *Mah jong* is a game played with a different kind of tiles. This game is popular in China, the Philippines, and Japan.

Objectives

- To introduce the concept that people around the world play similar games
- To familiarize children with two popular games, Go Fish and Dominoes.
- To introduce children to a game from China—Tiu-ü

Materials

Playing cards or Go Fish game cards, dominoes, *A to Z Poster*, copies of page 119 (one per child), *World Map*, string, thumbtack or tape, *Greetings Poster*

Introduction

Bring out a set of dominoes and see what games children like to play with them. Have children demonstrate alone, in pairs, or in groups how they like to play with the numbered tiles.

Later, have children play Go Fish. Play one game with children, explaining the rules with the cards face up. Then deal cards out face down, seven cards to each of three players, five cards to each of four or more players. The rest of the cards go face down in the center. Players look at their cards and arrange them in pairs: sixes, queens, aces, and so on. Four of a kind is a "book" and must be laid down in front of the player. The player on the dealer's left goes first, asking for cards he needs to make a book. He can ask any other player for a card(s). For example: *"Do you have any sixes?"* If the other player has sixes, that player must turn them over to the "asker." Then the "asker" can call for something else from that player or another player. If the other player has no sixes, she says: *"Go Fish,"* and the "asker" must take a card from the pile in the center. The next

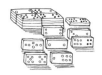

"asker" is the person on the first player's left. The winner is the first person to get rid of all his cards.

Working with the Poster

Tell children that in China people play a game that uses numbered tiles like dominoes and has rules that are very similar to Go Fish. Highlight the Tiu'ü game on the *A to Z Poster*. Have children compare the tiles with their dominoes. Then give each child a copy of page 119, so that they can take it home and share this new game with their families.

Help children find China on the *World Map*. Put a copy of the large illustration on the side of the *World Map*, and attach it to China with string.

See if children can remember how to greet each other in Chinese. (*"Ni hao."*) Challenge them to find the phrase on the *Greetings Poster*.

Follow-Up Activities

Math: Teach children how to play Tiu-ü. This game will help them develop their counting skills.

Social Studies: Invite grandparents and senior citizens to your class. Ask them to share some table games that they enjoyed playing as children. Some multicultural games that may come up are: Chinese Checkers, Parcheesi (India), and Mankala (Africa).

Art: Make a card game using the pictures on the *A to Z Poster*. Make two copies of each picture (or a reduction of the black-and-white illustrations). Paste the pictures on file cards. Place the 52 cards face down on a table or the floor. Have children find pairs, using the same rules as Concentration. To make the game more challenging, have children name the pictures. You may wish to add cards with other interesting objects to identify.

Social Studies: Help children learn more about contemporary China with books such as *Chasing the Moon to China,* by Virginia Overton McLean (Redbird Press).

Extending the Theme

Grandpa Tang's Story, by Ann Tombert (Crown), tells how a Chinese grandfather turns tangram puzzle pieces into animal illustrations to accompany his story.

Let's Color Korea. Traditional Games, by Mark Mueller (Hollym Corp.), describes many Korean games.

'Ud

Background Information

An *'ud* (OOD) is an Arabic lute. The lute is a stringed instrument, usually played by plucking. Some lutes, however, are played with a bow like a violin.

'Uds appeared in the Arab world about 4000 years ago. In the Middle Ages, Arabs introduced what is called the classical lute, and this instrument became popular in Europe during the Renaissance.

Today people throughout the world play lutes. In Greece, such an instrument is called a *bouzouki*. In Russia, people play the *balalaika*. In Portugal, it is called a *machete*. South Africans play a *ramkie*. Indians play the *sitar,* and Cambodians play the *cha pei*. These lutes differ in the length of the neck, the size of the belly, the number of strings, and the presence of frets (the ridges that cross the fingerboard.)

Objectives

* To introduce the concept that people all over the world play stringed instruments
* To familiarize children with some of the different sounds made by stringed instruments
* To familiarize children with one kind of stringed instrument—the 'ud

Materials

Various musical selections featuring stringed instruments (see below), *A to Z Poster,* black-and-white illustration on page 120, *World Map,* string, tape or thumbtack, *Greetings Poster*

Introduction

Play some musical selections for children that feature different stringed instruments. Suggestions include:
* *Peter and the Wolf,* by Prokfiev ("Peter's Theme")
* *Young Person's Guide to the Orchestra,* by Benjamin Britten (all instruments are highlighted)
* *Hush,* by Bobby McFerrin and Yo Yo Ma (cello is highlighted)
* "Elephant" from the *Carnival of Animals,* by Camille Saint-Saens (double bass is highlighted)
* *Dulcimer Lullaby,* by Joemy Wilson and Friends (dulcimer, guitar, violin, and celtic harp are highlighted)
* Selections from *Arab Music,* published by World Music Press (a recording with selections played on traditional instruments)

If possible, show pictures of the instruments as children listen to the music. End with a selection by an electric guitar. Tell children that the electric guitar is a modern instrument and has only been played for about 50 years.

Working with the Posters

Highlight the picture of the 'ud on the *A to Z Poster.* Then show children the black-and-white illustration of the 'ud. Talk about the shape of the instrument. Have children count the number of strings. Tell children that this type of stringed instrument has been played for 4000 years, in contrast to the electric guitar.

The 'ud is played in many countries in the Middle East and Africa. One country is Egypt. Find Egypt on the *World Map.* Put the picture on the side of the map, and attach it to Egypt with string.

In Egypt, as in many countries of the Middle East, people speak Arabic. Refer children to the *Greetings Poster,* and see if anyone can remember one way that people greet each other in Arabic. (*"As Salamu Alaykum."*) Challenge children to find the Arabic greeting on the poster.

Follow-Up Activities

Music/Art: Help children make box guitars.

Materials: boxes of various sizes like shoe boxes, cigar boxes, small cartons, rubber bands of various lengths and widths

What to Do:
1. Have each child choose a box and discard the top.
2. Then let him choose a variety of rubber bands that will stretch around the box.
3. Have children wrap their rubber bands around their boxes, leaving a 1-inch space between each band.
4. Show children how to pluck the rubber bands to create sounds.

Social Studies: Read *The Day of Ahmed's Secret* by Florence Parry Heide (Morrow), to help children learn something about a child's life in Egypt.

Music/Social Studies: Plan a Family Concert and invite family members to come to your class to play musical instruments. You could also take your class on a field trip to a high school or college music department or to a music store.

Extending the Theme

Dancing with the Indians, Angela Shelf Medearis (Scholastic), tells the story of a young girl who joins her family on a trip to a Seminole pow-wow.

Farid El Atrache: An Evening with the King of the Oud, (Digital Press/Hellas), is a recording of 'ud music, available in both cassette and CD.

 **Valero**

Background Information

Valero (vah-LAY-roh)) is a wooden stick-and-ball game from Mexico. A heavy string attaches the ball, in this case a solid cylinder with a hole in the middle, to the stick. The object of the game is to catch the wooden cylinder on the stick. In many cases, the cylinder is painted or carved.

This game of hand-eye coordination takes many forms in different parts of the world. The stick can be a cup, and the cylinder or ball can be rings. The Inuit people play a version called *ajaqaq*, made from the bones of animals, such as the walrus. Sioux children play with a cup, instead of a stick, attached with a leather string to a ball. Some Algonquin play a game at harvest time in which a ring is tossed onto the end of a corncob. People in Ecuador and Columbia play a game called *bolero* with a wooden stick and rings.

Objectives

* To show children how to make simple games
* To let children practice hand-eye coordination by playing a cup-and-ball game
* To introduce children to a cup-and-ball game played in Mexico—valero

Materials

7-or 9-ounce paper cup, masking tape, aluminum foil, string or yarn, hole puncher, *A to Z Poster,* black-and-white illustration on page 121, *World Map,* tape or thumbtack, *Greetings Poster*

Introduction

Make the following valero-style cup-and-ball game to share with children.
What to Do:

1. Crumple a piece of aluminum foil to create a "ball" that will fit in the paper cup.
2. Tie one end of 16-inch piece of string around the foil ball.
3. Poke a hole in the side of the cup, put the other end of the string through the hole and knot it so it is attached to the cup.
4. Flick the ball up with the wrist, and try to catch it in the cup.
5. Demonstrate how to play the game and then let children take turns trying it. Make games with different lengths of string. (The bigger the ball and the shorter the string, the easier the game.) Together make up rules for playing— number of tries per turn, etc.

Working with the Posters

Tell children that people all over the world play games similar to the one you made. Highlight the picture of the valero on the *A to Z Poster*. Show children the black-and-white illustration, and ask them how they think this game is played.

Tell children that valero is played in Mexico. Find Mexico on the *World Map*. Discuss how close the country is to the United States. Name the states that border Mexico. (California, Arizona, Texas) Put the picture of the valero on the side of the map, and attach it to Mexico with string.

Refer children to the *Greetings Poster*. See if anyone can remember a way that Spanish-speaking people greet each other. (*"¡Hola!"*) Point out the word on the poster.

Follow-Up Activities

Math: Make a chart and have children record with tally marks the number of times they can catch the ball in the cup in a given period of time. To make sure this is noncompetitive, have children keep personal charts and try to beat their own records, or have them compare the number of catches they make in different amounts of time rather than individual performances.

Art: Have children make their own cup-and-ball games, following the directions on the preceding page. Have children decorate their paper cups before making the game. Let them brush liquid starch or diluted white glue on tissue paper and then layer it on the cup. The colors will run together. Let the cup dry thoroughly before poking the hole in the side.

Social Studies: Invite families to share games that they enjoyed as children. Make a game exhibit for your classroom.

Social Studies: Read a book, such as *Treasure Nap*, by Juanita Havil (Houghton Mifflin), to learn more about life in Mexico.

Extending the Theme

Galimoto, by Karen Lee Williams, (Lothrop, Lee & Shepard), tells the story of a young boy in Malawi who creates a toy from scraps and throwaways.

A World of Toys, by Della Rowland (Contemporary Books), tells about toys from many cultures.

Wycinanki

Background Information

Wycinanki (vee-chee-NAN-kee) is the Polish name for paper cut designs. Based on traditional decorations painted both on the inside and outside walls of buildings and on furniture, the first wycinanki were simple designs usually cut from ordinary writing paper by farm families. The earliest tool was sheep shears. The first designs were primarily seasonal in theme, often related to holidays.

As wycinanki became a true folk art, distinctive designs developed in different areas of Poland, often incorporating elements from nature or scenes from peasant life. One of the best-known modern styles comes from the Kurpie district of Poland. It is a symmetrical design cut from a single piece of colored paper, folded once, with spruce trees and birds as a common motif. Another style from Lovitz, a Polish city, uses many layers of brightly colored paper assembled on a basic cutting, usually black.

People of many cultures have developed distinctive crafts with paper folding and cutting: *kirigami* or *mon-kiri* in Japan, *scherenschnitte* in Germany.

Objectives

* To introduce the concept that all over the world ordinary people, not just professional artists, create works of art. These works of art are called folk art.
* To familiarize children with one type of folk art—wycinanki
* To give children experiences with some of the basic elements of wycinanki: symmetry, layered papers, contrasting colors

Materials

Scissors, different colored pieces of construction paper, crayons, markers, *A to Z Poster,* black-and-white illustration on page 122, *World Map,* string, tape or thumbtack, *Greetings Poster,* file card or sticky-back note

Introduction

Fold a piece of paper in half and draw half of a symmetrical shape, such as a heart. Ask children to predict what the shape will be when it is cut out. Repeat the process with another simple shape. Ask children to suggest other shapes/objects that will be the same on both sides. Try out their suggestions. Then let them try to cut out similar shapes. Let children paste the shapes on a large piece of paper to create a class collage.

Introduce children to the word *symmetrical*, which means that two sides of a figure are exactly alike. Tell them that you are going to show them a special craft in which symmetrical shapes are very important.

Working with the Posters

Highlight the picture of the wycinanki on the *A to Z Poster*. Explain to children that an adult artist using scissors cut out this design. Point out the artist's use of bright colors and layering.

Then show children the large illustration of the wycinanki. Talk about the design. Ask children what shapes they see. Help children identify symmetrical shapes.

Tell children that wycinanki is a traditional craft in Poland. Locate Poland on the *World Map*. Attach the picture to the side of the map. Put a string from the picture to the country.

One way children in Poland greet each other is by saying: *"Czesc."* (CHESCH)   Add the greeting to the *Greetings Poster*.

Follow-Up Activities

Art: Help children make their own versions of wycinanki.

Materials: 8- or 10-inch paper doilies (one per child); assorted colored construction paper; cut into 4-by-4-inch squares; scissors; glue; 12-by-18-inch construction paper

What to Do:
1. Give each child a paper square. Demonstrate how to fold the paper in half and cut out symmetrical shapes. Let children do this several times with various pieces of paper, making different-sized shapes. Let children cut out non-symmetrical shapes if they wish.
2. Give each child a doily. The doily will become the base for each paper cutting. Have children examine it to see if it is symmetrical. Have them glue their shapes onto the doily, creating layers.
3. Mount the decorated doily on a contrasting color of construction paper.

Children's Literature: Explore picture books illustrated with paper cuts; for example, the books of Leo Lionni, Eric Carle, and Giles LaRoche.

Math: Create a matching game on unruled index cards. Fold cards, and draw and cut out halves of symmetrical shapes. Let children put the shapes together.

Social Studies: Help children learn more about Poland by looking at the pictures in books, such as *Poland (Enchantment of the World Series),* by Carol Greene (Children's Press).

Extending the Theme

Crafts of Many Cultures, by Aurelia Gomez (Scholastic), is a resource book with multicultural crafts, including wycinanki.

Xylophone

Background Information

A xylophone is a musical instrument that is made of a set of wooden bars, graduated by pitch, set parallel to one another in a frame. In order to make a sound, the bars must be struck with a stick or club. Most xylophones also have a resonator, a hollow chamber, either under each bar or under the whole instrument. When the bar is struck, it vibrates, and the vibrations set the air in the resonator moving, creating a hollow tone that makes the sound louder.

Different forms of xylophones are played in many cultures. The large log xylophones of Guinea consist of a number of logs resting on the musician's outstretched legs. The *mbila* of South Africa has tin-can resonators, and the *marimbas* of Central America have carved wooden resonators. In Southeast Asia, a cradle-shaped resonator is most often used in xylophones such as the *rang nat* of Laos and the *roneat ek* of Cambodia. In the United States, xylophones used in orchestras consist of two rows of wooden bars (arranged as a piano keyboard) suspended over hollow tube resonators.

Objectives

- To introduce the concept that different materials make different sounds when struck
- To introduce children to a musical instrument played in many cultures—the xylophone
- To familiarize children with one type of xylophone—a wood-and-gourd xylophone from Sierra Leone

Materials

Glasses or soda bottles, water, paper towel, spoon, toy xylophone, *A to Z Poster*, black-and-white illustration on page 123, *World Map*, string, tape or thumbtack, *Greetings Poster*, file card or sticky-back note

Introduction

Introduce the concept of musical instruments that are struck and make noise through a resonator with the following activity.

Make a musical instrument by lining up four empty glasses or soda bottles on a paper towel. Fill each to a different level with water. Let children tap the glasses or bottles with a spoon. Ask children to guess why the sounds are different. Let them experiment with making different sounds and perhaps trying to play a simple tune.

Working with the Posters

If possible, let children experiment with a toy xylophone, making loud and soft sounds. Point out the materials from which the instrument is made. There are many different types of xylophones around the world. Highlight the picture of the xylophone on the *A to Z Poster*. Then show children the black-and-white illustration of the musical instrument. Tell children that this xylophone is made of wooden bars under which are gourds. Sometimes there are small holes in the sides of the gourds with thin coverings made from the egg cases of spiders. (If you have read the story about Anansi on page 126, you can remind children that spiders are important folklore characters in West Africa.) These coverings add a "buzz" to the sound of the xylophone.

These xylophones are played in Sierra Leone. Locate this West African country on the *World Map*. Attach the picture of the xylophone on the side of the map. Put a string from the picture to Sierra Leone.

The official language of Sierra Leone is English. Help children find other countries in the world where English is the most common language spoken.

Follow-Up Activities

Science: Wind chimes operate on the same principle as the xylophone. When the chimes strike each other, they vibrate and create sounds. Let children experiment making wind chimes using a wire coat hanger (cover wire tip with tape) or a wooden dowel as a base. Have them hang various objects on the base by attaching one end of a piece of string to the object and tying the other end around the base. Objects might include different-sized metal spoons, aluminum pie plates with holes punched in one end, or different lengths of aluminum tubing. Hang the chimes by an open window or outside on a low branch and let children listen to the different sounds.

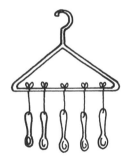

Music: Create a class rhythm band with a shekere (see pages 84-85), drums, xylophones (let children take turns "playing" the water glasses), and any other percussion instruments or shakers you have in the music area.

Social Studies: Help children learn more about African cultures with books such as *Ashanti to Zulu: African Traditions,* by Margaret Musgrove (Dial); *Moja Means One,* by Muriel Feelings (Dial); and *Africa Brothers and Sisters,* by Virginia Kroll (Four Winds).

Extending the Theme

Chaminuka: Mbira and Marimba Music of Zimbabwe, by Dumisani Maraire (World Music Press), is a tape of original and traditional music.

Yeon

Background Information

Yeon (yahn) are Korean kites. People of all ages in Korea from children to the highest government officials fly colorful kites. However, yeon are only flown during a certain period of time—the first half of the first month of the lunar year. After this time, if anyone should fly a yeon, he would be laughed at. In Korea, no one will even touch a lost kite after mid-January.

On the fourteenth day of the first month, it is customary to write a message on paper and attach it to the yeon. This message carries the wish: "Evil be gone. Blessings welcome." Mothers write the message for their young children along with the child's name and date of birth. These kites are flown high and then released.

Korean kites tend to be rectangular, from 15 to 20 inches long. The string is attached to the kite and to a large kite reel.

Kite flying is a popular pastime in many cultures. In Japan, some kites or *tako* are tiny; others are up to eighteen feet across. In France, one type of kite is called *cerf volant,* or "flying stag." In Thailand, men's kites, *chula*, are shaped like a five-pointed star, representing the five senses and the five fingers. Kites flown by Thai women, *pakpao*, are diamond-shaped.

Objectives

- To introduce children to the idea that people in many countries fly kites
- To have children explore the conditions necessary for kite flying
- To familiarize children with one type of kite—yeon

Materials

Chart paper, markers, *A to Z Poster,* black-and-white illustration on page 122, *World Map,* string, tape or thumbtacks, *Greetings Poster,* file card or sticky-back note

Introduction

Ask children if anyone has ever flown a kite. Have children describe kites they have seen. Make a list of conditions and materials that are necessary for kite flying. Look out the window and ask children whether it is a good day for kite flying. Discuss why it is or isn't a good day.

Talk about the importance of wind for activities, such as sailing, playing with pinwheels, and wind surfing.

Working with the Posters

Tell children that since wind is part of the weather all around the world, kite flying is a popular sport in many countries. Highlight the yeon on the *A to Z Poster*. Tell children that this kite is flown only at a special time of the year. It comes from Korea. Show children the black-and-white illustration. Talk about the picture on the kite.

Find Korea on the *World Map,* and put the picture of the yeon beside the map. Attach the picture to the country with string.

Tell children that one way Korean people greet each other is by saying, "Yo-bo-se-yo." You may wish to add this to the *Greetings Poster.*

여보세요

Follow-Up Activities

Art/Science: Help children make their own kites.

Materials: lunch-sized paper bags, scissors, hole puncher, string, markers and crayons, crepe paper streamers

What to Do:

1. Cut off bottom of bag.
2. Mark lines as shown in Diagram A. Cut along lines on one side of bag only.
3. Open triangle flaps to the side. Cut out a triangle "vent" in the center of the bag. Punch one hole in each wing flap. (See Diagram B)

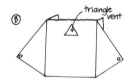

4. Have children decorate kites and add crepe paper streamers.
5. Tie a piece of string to both holes. Knot the two free ends together and attach a single piece of string (3 to 4 ft.) to the knot. (See Diagram C)
6. Take kites outside to an open area on a windy day and let children run with them until they are aloft.

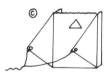

Social Studies: Help children learn more about life in Korea with a book such as *Chi-Hook, A Korean Girl,* by Patricia McMahon (Caroline House).

Extending the Theme

Gilberto and the Wind, by Marie Hall Ets (Puffin), is the story of a Hispanic boy who explores what the wind can do.

The Emperor and The Kite, by Jane Yolen (Philomel), tells of a tiny Chinese princess who saves the Emperor with the help of a special kite.

Dragon Kite of the Autumn Moon, by Valerie Reddix (Lothrop, Lee, & Shepard), tells of a Chinese boy and his grandfather who make a special kite and fly it together until the year Grandfather becomes ill.

Zampoña

Background Information

Zampoña (tham-POH-nyah) is a Spanish word meaning "panpipes." This musical instrument is made of hollow tubes of different lengths, tied together in a row. The sound is made by the vibrating columns of air, created when you blow across the tops of the tubes. Made of clay, stone, cane, wood, metal, or plastic, they were first associated with the ancient Greek God, Pan. Panpipes were played in ancient Peru. The zampoña is a still popular Peruvian instrument.

There are three basic forms of panpipes: raft panpipes, bundle panpipes, and double panpipes. Panpipes are found in many countries around the world, including China, where they are called *p'ai hsiao*; Germany—*fotzhobel*; Turkey—*mithqal*; and Egypt—*sa fa fir*.

Objectives

- To introduce the concept that people all over the world make music with flutes
- To help children understand how flutes make music
- To familiarize children with one special type of flute—the panpipe or zampoña

Materials

Five clean, empty glass soda bottles of assorted sizes, water, *A to Z Poster,* black-and-white illustration on page 125, *World Map,* string, tape or thumbtack, *Greetings Poster*

Introduction

Introduce children to the way flutes make music with the following activities.
What to Do:
1. Display five glass soda bottles—one large, one small, and three of the same size. Ask children to guess how you could make sounds using the empty bottles. Try out various ideas, including tapping the bottles with a spoon, blowing into a bottle.
2. Blow over a large bottle and a small one. Discuss the difference in sounds.
3. Now line up three bottles of the same size. Leave one bottle empty, add a little water to one bottle, and add more water to the last bottle. Blow over the tops of each bottle. Have children compare the sounds.
4. Invite children to try making sounds by blowing across the tops of bottles. This can be difficult, so try it in small groups, and give children lots of opportunity to practice. Be sure the bottles are rinsed and wiped clean after each child's turn.

Working with the Posters

Introduce children to zampoñas by highlighting the panpipe on the *A to Z Poster.* Then show children the black-and-white illustration. Have children count the number of tubes they see. Explain that the zampoña player makes sounds in the same way as they did on the soda bottles, by blowing over the reeds, except that the zampoña is usually played by blowing across the top of all the reeds at the same time.

Zampoñas are played in many countries; one of these is Peru. Find Peru on the *World Map,* and then affix the large illustration to the edge of the poster. Attach the picture to Peru with string or yarn.

Tell children that many people in Peru speak Spanish. See if anyone can tell how children in Peru would greet each other. (*"¡Hola!"*) Refer to the *Greetings Poster* as a reminder.

Follow-Up Activities

Science/Music: Help children learn about how vibrations cause sound by making kazoos.

Materials: (per child) 1 cardboard tube (from bathroom tissue or paper towel roll), 1 rubber band, one 6-by-6-inch piece of waxed paper

What to Do:

1. Have each child cover one end of the cardboard tube with waxed paper and secure it in place with the rubber band.
2. Have children gently hum into the tube. The vibrating waxed paper will produce a sound.
3. Then have each child put a hand on the paper (so it doesn't vibrate) and hum. No vibrating sound will be made.
4. Form a kazoo orchestra. Have children choose tunes to be hummed.

Music: Invite a parent, teacher, or music student into your class to play the flute for children.

Social Studies: Share information and pictures about Peru with books such as *Tonight Is Carnaval* by Arthur Dorros (Dutton).

Extending the Theme

Flute Player, by Michael Lacapa (Northland Publishers), retells the old Apache folktale of a flute player and young woman whose lives touch for a moment in time.

The Singing Snake, by Stefan Czenecki and Timothy Rhodes (Hyperion), is a folktale about the origin of the Australianmusical instrument, the *didgeridoo.*

Anansi

Multicultural Poster Program

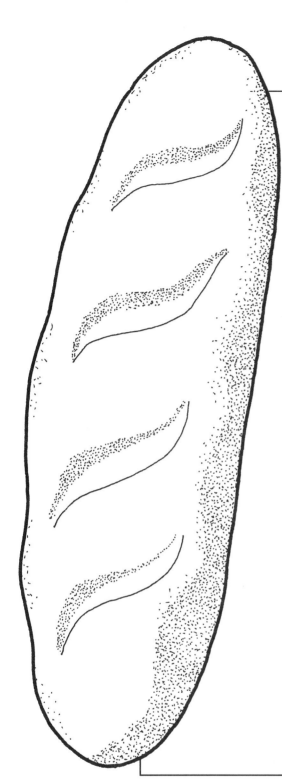

Time: Allot 20 minutes for dough-making, 2 hours and 15 minutes rising time, and 1 hour baking.

Ingredients: 2 envelopes yeast, 1/3 C lukewarm water, 1 T sugar, 4 C white flour, 1 1/2 T salt, 1 C lukewarm water, cornmeal for the pan, 1 egg white, 2 T water

What to Do:

1. Let children mix the 1/3 cup warm water with the sugar.
2. Stir the yeast into the sugar-water mixture.
3. Help children put the flour in a large mixing bowl.
4. Make a well in the center of the flour and stir in the yeast mixture, adding enough of the remaining lukewarm water to incorporate all the flour.
5. Let children knead the mixture for 4 or 5 minutes, then put the bowl in a pan of warm water, cover it with a tea towel, and let the dough rise 2 hours.
6. Punch it down for 2 minutes, then divide the dough into 2 parts. Stretch and roll each part into a long baguette, 1 1/2 inches in diameter.
7. Sprinkle baking sheet with cornmeal and lay baguettes down.
8. Let baguettes rise 15 minutes. Score them 5 or 6 times diagonally with a knife and put them in a cold oven.
9. Set oven at 350°F and bake baguettes for 1 hour.
10. Place a pan of hot water on the oven floor for a crisp crust. Remove halfway through baking.
11. Ten minutes before the baguettes are done, paint them with an egg white beaten with 2 T water.

Baguette

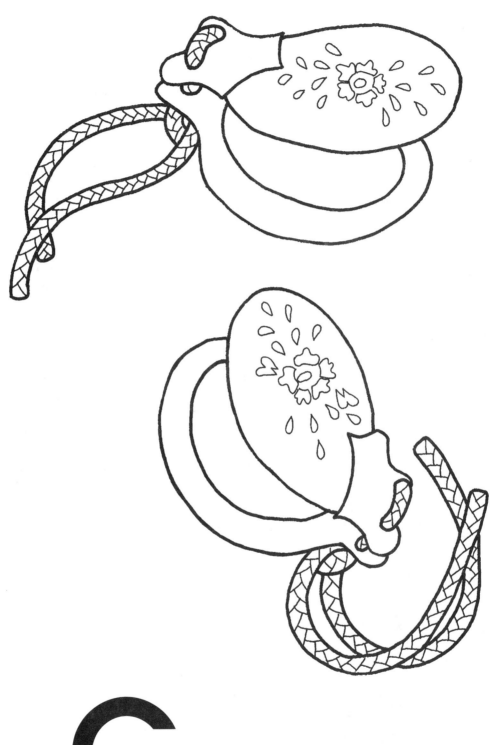

Castanets

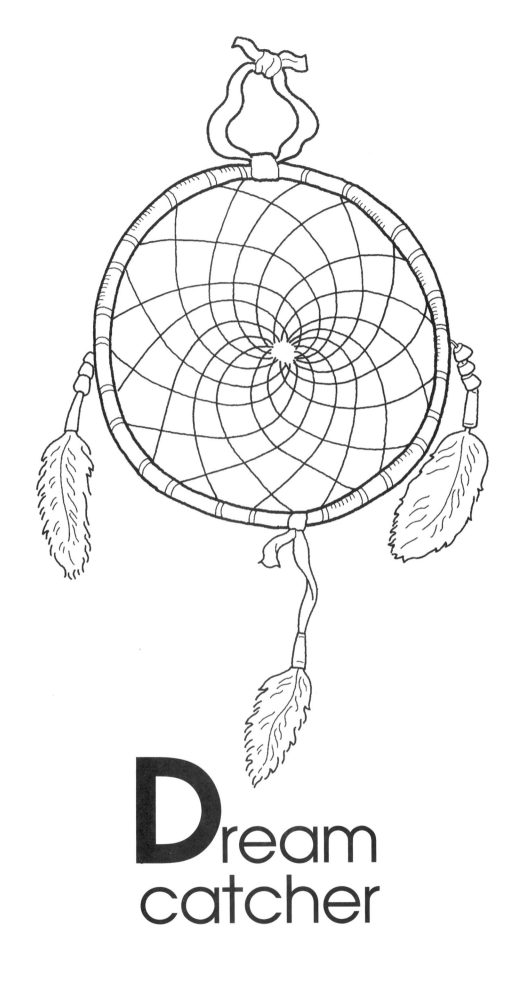

Dream catcher

Elephant

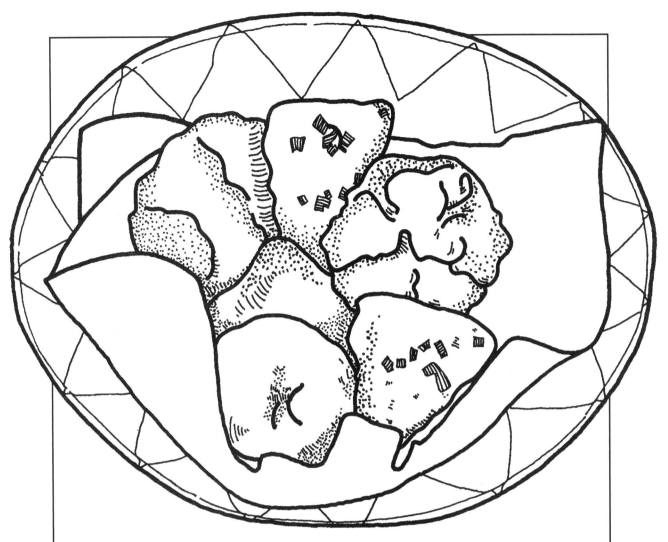

Ingredients: 3 C unbleached flour, 2 t baking powder (increase to 3 t at high altitudes), 1 t salt, 1 1/2 C warm water or milk, 1 T oil or shortening

What to Do:

1. Help children combine all ingredients except oil and knead until smooth.
2. Have children rub oil or shortening over dough.
3. Cover the dough and let it sit 30 minutes.
4. Either pat or roll out enough dough to fit in the palm of child's hand in a circle about 1/ 8-inch thick.
5. Deep fry the circles in hot oil or shortening. (ADULT ONLY)
   Makes 10-12 fry breads.

Fry bread

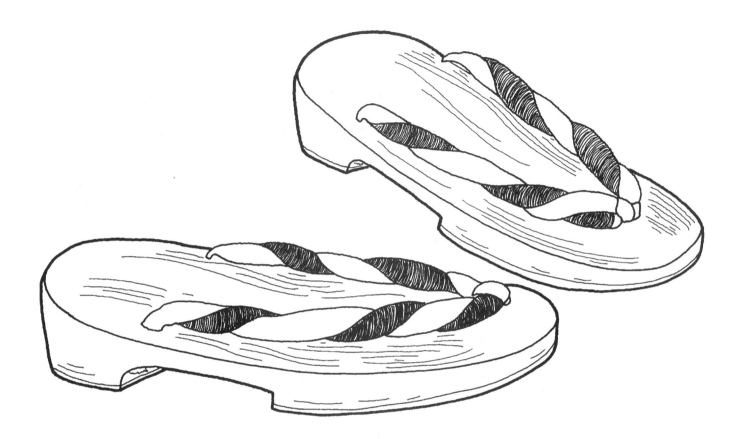

Geta

Hop-round

bheque

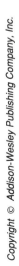

Junk

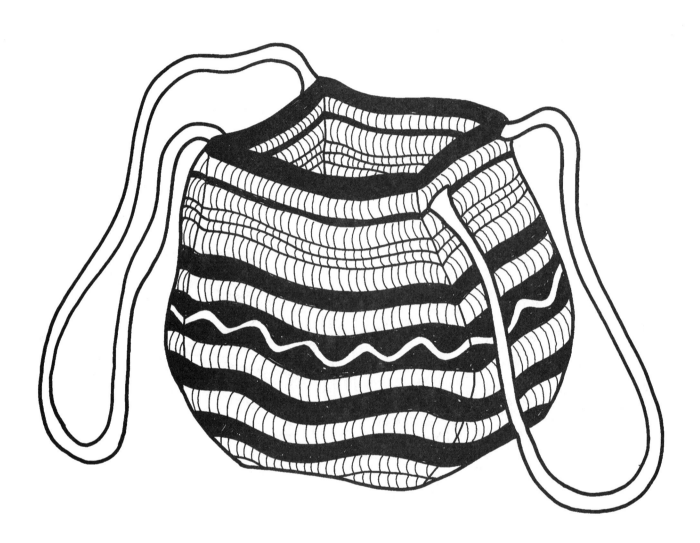

Kiondo

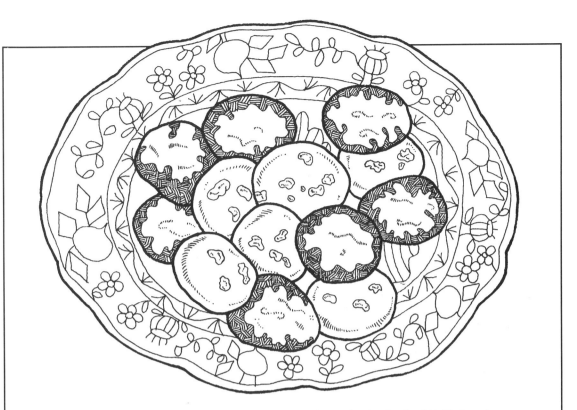

Ingredients: 3 C self-rising flour, 2 t ground allspice, pinch of salt, 1/4 C clear honey, 1 C packed dark brown sugar, 3 T butter, 1 beaten egg, finely grated peel of 1 lemon, 1 T lemon juice, 8 oz semisweet chocolate (melted), 1 egg white, 1 1/2 C sifted powdered sugar

What to Do:

1. Preheat oven to 350°F (175°C).
2. Grease a large baking sheet with butter.
3. Sift flour, allspice, and salt into a large bowl; make a well in the center.
4. Put honey, brown sugar, and butter in a small saucepan; stir over low heat until melted. Cool slightly.
5. Pour melted mixture into well of dry ingredients; add beaten egg, lemon peel, and juice; mix to form a soft dough.
6. Knead on a floured surface until smooth. Roll out dough. Using cookie cutters, cut dough into desired shapes.
7. Bake cookies 20 to 25 minutes or until lightly browned. Remove to wire rack. Cool.
8. When cool, place rack over a large baking sheet; coat cookies with melted chocolate. Allow chocolate to set.
9. In a medium-size bowl, beat egg white with powdered sugar until stiff peaks are formed.
10. Decorate cookies, simply or elaborately, with sugar icing.

Lebkuchen

Matroshka dolls

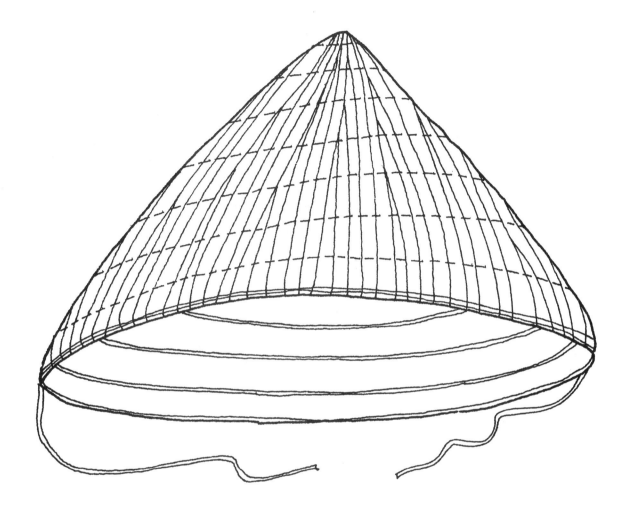

Non la

Ofrenda
pictures

Ingredients: 3 C sweet rice or long grain white rice, 5 C unsweetened coconut milk, 1 small coconut, grated, 1 C sugar

What to Do:
1. Let children help wash the rice and put it in a 2-quart sauce pan or kettle with cover.
2. Add coconut milk and cook over high heat until steam escapes from under the edge of the cover. Lower heat and allow to steam until cooked.
3. Mold each serving in a coffee cup. Unmold into the coffee cup saucer. Sprinkle sugar and grated coconut on top of each serving.

Palay

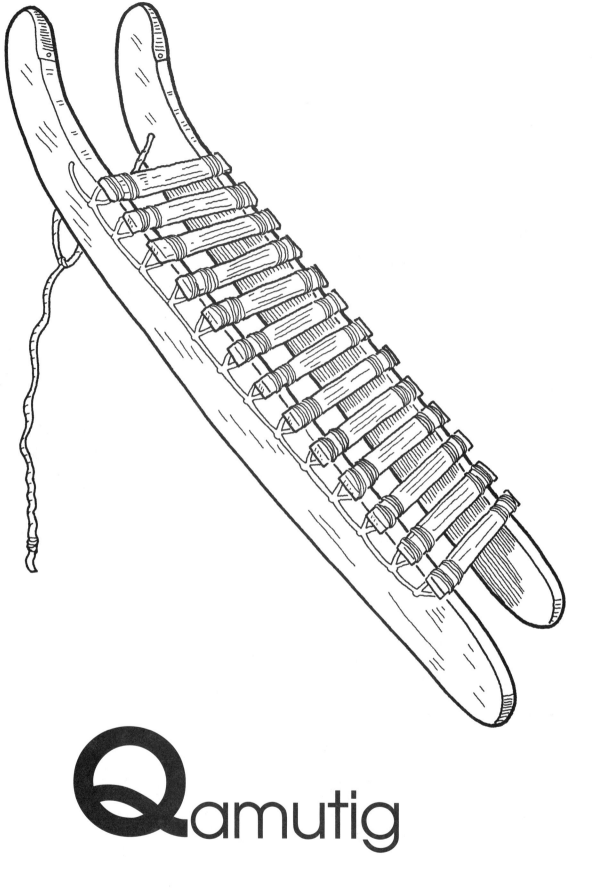

Qamutig

Raven

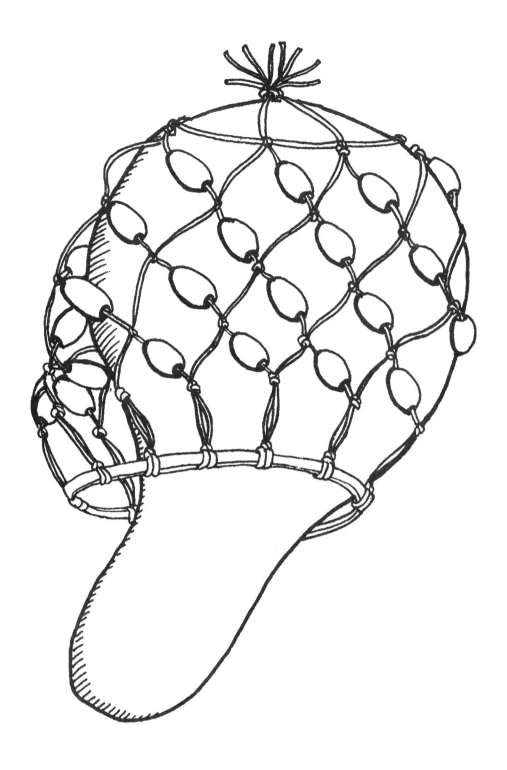

Shekere

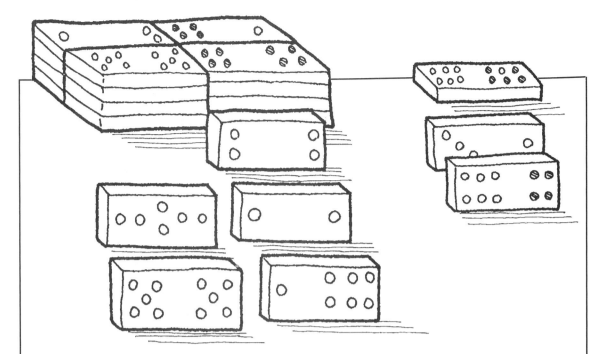

Materials: Chinese or American dominoes (64 tiles)

How to Play:
This game combines the rules of Go Fish with the playing pieces or tiles for Dominoes. Here's how to play.

1. Place the tiles face down in a "woodpile" of 16 stacks of four tiles each. Take four stacks of four tiles from one end of the pile and place the stacks face up in the center of the table.

2. If there are two players, each draws three stacks from the woodpile and sets up the 12 tiles facing her or him. (Three players each draw two stacks.)

3. The players examine their tiles. Any pair of double sixes is laid out immediately on the table.

4. Then the first player tries to match (with the same number of spots) one of her tiles with one that is face up in the center stack on the table. If she succeeds, she places the pair in front of her on the table. She then draws a tile from the top of the woodpile and tries to match this tile with one of those face up next to the center stack.

5. The next player in turn tries to match one of his tiles with one that is face up. If he is successful, he draws from the woodpile, and so on, until there are no more tiles in the woodpile.

6. At the end of the game, players count their scores according to the value of each tile they have in front of them in a pair. (Younger children can count tiles instead of spots.)

Tiu-ü

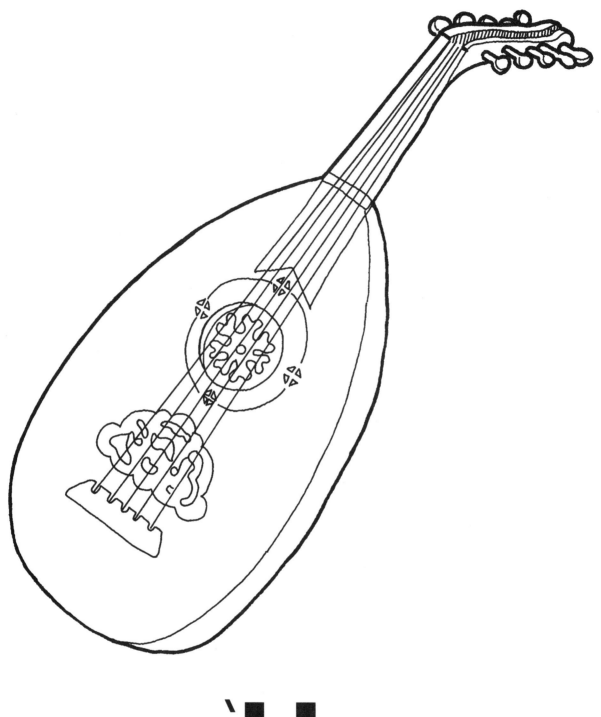

`U_d

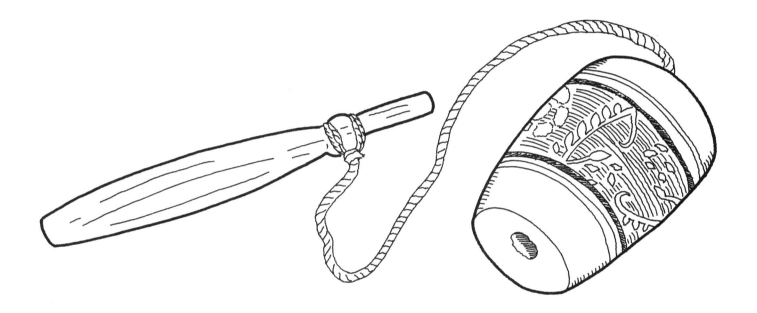

Valero

Wycinanki

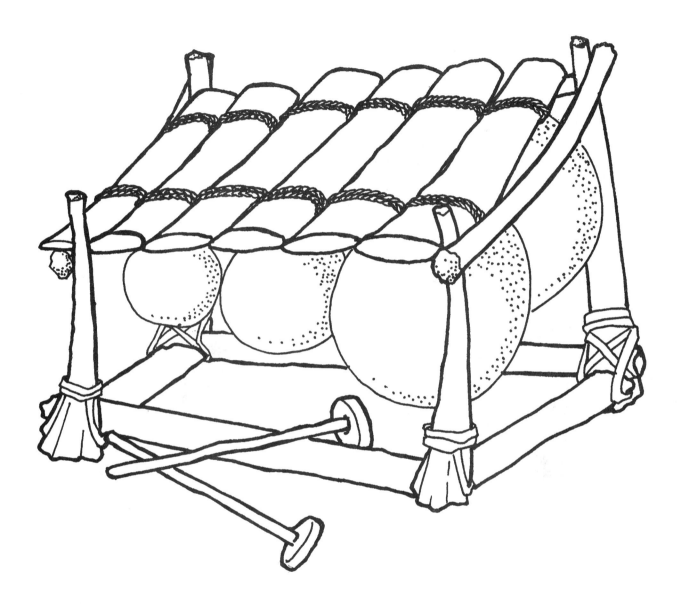

Xylophone

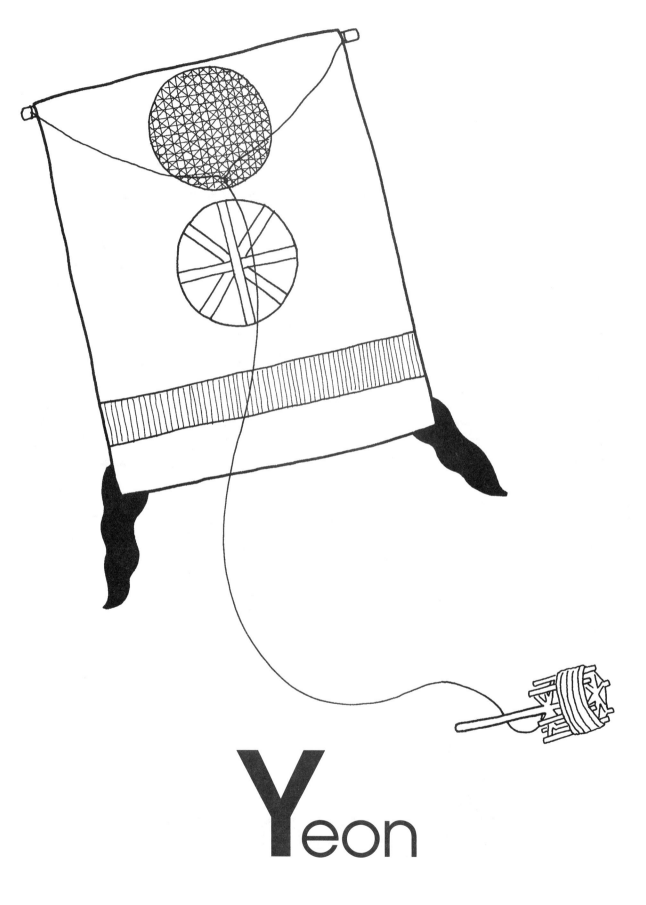

Yeon

Multicultural Poster Program

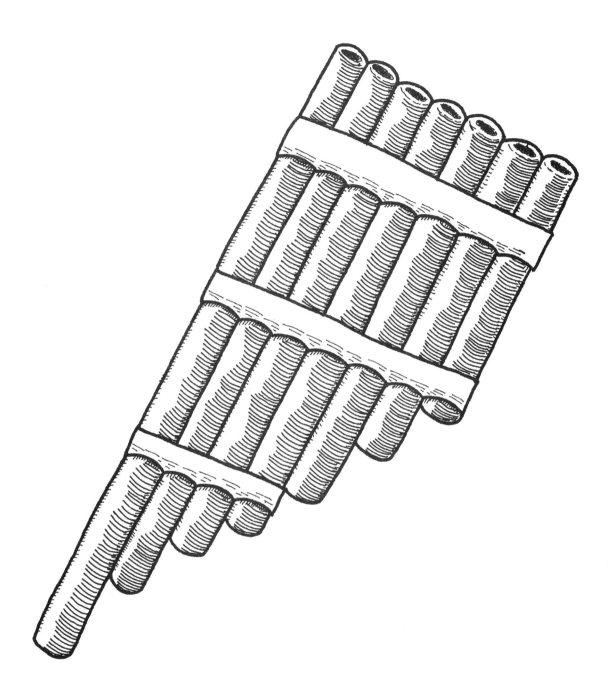

Zampoña

Anansi and the Pot of Wisdom

When the world was very young, the sky god, Nyame, had all the wisdom in the world, and he gave it to Anansi to do with as he pleased. Now Anansi was a greedy fellow, and he decided to keep all the wisdom for himself. *"Someday, I will become king,"* he said to himself. *"For I will be the only wise person in the whole world. But now I must hide the wisdom, so no one else will get it and become wise."*

Anansi got a giant clay pot and stuffed the wisdom inside, covering the pot tightly, so no good sense could get out. Then he went into the jungle to find a place to hide the pot.

Anansi ran swiftly through the jungle. All the animals wanted to know where he was going in such a hurry. But Anansi didn't stop to answer their questions. He just kept looking for a good hiding place.

Suddenly, Anansi had a clever idea. *"I'll hide the pot in the tallest tree in the world—a place where no one will find my wisdom."*

Anansi looked until he found the tallest tree in the jungle—in fact, the tallest tree in the whole world. It was the giant silk-cotton tree. It had huge roots coming out of the ground, roots that were large enough to hide an elephant. It had a smooth, wide trunk, and at the top its branches spread out, covered with silver leaves and a filmy cotton-like gauze.

Anansi was delighted with the tree. *"No one but me will be able to climb the wide, smooth trunk, and there are no branches near the ground!"* He laughed.

Anansi brought the pot of wisdom back to the bottom of the tree. Even though the outside of tree was smooth as silk, the spider was sure that he could climb it. Anansi was very proud. He had more legs than almost any creature in the world. Animals have four legs, and people have only two legs, but Anansi had eight legs!

Anansi hung the pot right in front of himself by tying it around his neck with a piece of strong rope. Then he started to climb, using four of his legs to move and four to hold the heavy pot. He had to go slowly, but he started moving up the tree. Then suddenly, he slipped and fell all the way to the ground. He started again and again, but each time he fell down.

Anansi was getting warm, tired—and angry! Now Anansi was really angry. His eldest son, Kuma, had been watching all the time. *"Father, why don't you hang the pot behind you instead of in front?"* He suggested. *"Then you will be able to climb the tree."*

Anansi thought his son's suggestion was very wise. Suddenly, he realized that he didn't have all the wisdom in the world if his son was so wise. The spider was so angry that he hurled the pot onto the ground. It made a great noise and broke apart. The wisdom poured out. People and animals heard the noise and came from everywhere to see what it was. When they saw the wisdom on the ground, everyone took some of it. In fact, they spread it all around the world, and that is why there is so much good sense in the world, enough for everyone, for you and for me.

How Raven Stole the Sun

Long, long ago, the world was completely dark. There was no sun in the sky. This was because high above in the heavens, a powerful chief kept the fiery ball hidden away in a beautiful carved box. He would share the sun with no one.

Now on the dark earth, Raven was very hungry, but he could find no food because he couldn't see. So one day Raven decided to bring sunlight to the earth.

Raven realized that he would have to steal the sun, since the chief refused to share it. Raven watched the chief's house and discovered that each day the daughter of the chief went to a spring to get a drink of water. One day, he turned himself into a leaf and floated into her drinking cup. But just as she started to drink, the chief's daughter saw the leaf and threw it into the spring.

Next, Raven turned himself into a pine needle and floated down into the cup. But the suspicious daughter threw out the pine needle as soon as she noticed it.

Then Raven changed into a tiny grain of sand, so small that the chief's daughter never noticed it when she dipped her cup in the spring and drank. She never knew that she had swallowed Raven!

Some time later, the chief's daughter learned that she was going to have a baby. It was really Raven inside of her stomach! And when the baby (Raven) was born, the chief and his daughter loved the child.

But this baby was always unhappy. No matter how they tried to make it happy, the baby just cried. It cried and cried, even though the chief gave his grandchild every toy and every plaything he could think of, the baby grew more unhappy every day.

One day the baby screamed for the carved box which held the sun. The chief didn't want to give up his prize, but he loved the baby. Finally he gave the fiery ball to the child in the hope that it would stop crying.

Immediately, the baby changed back into Raven, who snatched the sun in his beak and flew out of the house through the chimney.

Away Raven soared, far into the heavens, for he was being chased by the chief, who became furious when he realized that he had been tricked. Soon Raven found that it was difficult to fly very fast because the sun was so heavy, so he broke off some pieces. When he threw the pieces into the sky, they became the moon, the stars, and the planets.

The chief was still following Raven, getting closer and closer, as Raven came in sight of the earth. Just before he landed on Earth, Raven threw the fiery ball up into the sky, and in a huge flash of light, it became the sun. A great cheer went up from all of the creatures on Earth. They celebrated because for the first time they had enough light to find food.

But because he had carried the sun such a long way, poor Raven's body was scorched by the fiery ball. And that is why Raven's feathers are black today.

Resources for Teachers

Catalogs

- Claudia's Caravan P. O. Box 1582, Alameda, CA 94501 Specializes in multicultural/multilingual books, recordings, games, and artifacts.
- Econo-Clad Books, P. O. Box 1777, Topeka, KS 66601 An excellent multicultural/multiethnic book catalog for grades K–12.
- Kit Rental Department, The Children's Museum, 300 Congress Street, Boston, MA 02210-1034 Multi-media interdisciplinary teaching units with one to three week lesson plans for cultural studies. Free brochure available.
- Savanna Books, 1132 Massachusetts Avenue, Cambridge, MA 02138 A bookstore and resource center specializing in books about children of color.
- Talking Drum, 1132 Massachusetts Avenue, Cambridge, MA 02138 Reference Person: Deborah Lotus. A store and resource center specializing in African and tribal arts, percussion instruments, and authentic artifacts.
- The National Storytelling Resource Center (NAPPS) P.O. Box 309, Jonesborough, Tennessee 37659. Storytellers who will visit schools are listed in the *National Directory of Storytelling*, (#N180) available for $3.00.
- World Music Press, P.O. Box 2565 Danbury, CT 06813 A publisher and distributor of World Music Press Titles, multicultural book and tape sets, and authentic ethnic chorale pieces.

Books for Teachers

Anti-Bias Curriculum: Tools for Empowering Young Children, by Louise Derman Sparks and the ABC Task Force (NAEYC)

Art From Many Hands, by Jo Miles Shuman (Davis Publications)

Cultural Awareness for Children, by Judy Allen, Earldene McNeill, and Velma Schmidt (Addison-Wesley)

The Book of Cookies, by Pat Alburey (HP Books)

Explorations With Young Children: A Curriculum Guide from the Bank Street College of Education, edited by Anne Michell and Judy David (Gryphon House)

Games from Many Lands, by Anita Benarde (Lion Press)

Globalchild, by Maureen Cech (Addison-Wesley)

Games of the World: How to Make Them, How to Play Them, and How They Came to Be, by Frederic V. Grunfeld (Swiss Committee for UNICEF)

Musical Instruments of the World, by Diagram Group (Paddington Press)

Simple Folk Instruments to Make and Play, by Ilene Hunter and Marilyn Judson (Simon & Schuster)

The Paper Design Cut-Out Book, by Ramona Jablonski (Stemmer House)

Spirit of the Harvest (a Native American cookbook), by Beverly Cox and Martin Jacobs (Stewart, Tabori, & Chang)